D0956610

# A SUMMER
# WITH MONTAIGNE

Antoine Compagnon

# A SUMMER
# WITH MONTAIGNE

*Translated from the French
by Tina Kover*

Europa
*editions*

Europa Editions
214 West 29th Street
New York, N.Y. 10001
www.europaeditions.com
info@europaeditions.com

Translation by Tina Kover
Original title: *Un été avec Montaigne*
Translation copyright © 2019 by Europa Editions

Library of Congress Cataloging in Publication Data is available
ISBN 978-1-60945-530-9

Compagnon, Antoine
A Summer with Montaigne

Book design and cover illustration by Emanuele Ragnisco
www.mekkanografici.com

Cover illustration taken from an image at Alamy Stock Photo

Prepress by Grafica Punto Print – Rome

Printed in the USA

# CONTENTS

# A SUMMER
# WITH MONTAIGNE

"People would be lying on the beach, or sipping cocktails, getting ready to have lunch, and they'd hear you chatting about Montaigne on the radio." When Philippe Val asked me to give a short talk about *Essays* on France Inter every weekday for the span of a summer, the idea seemed quite bizarre to me, and the challenge of it so risky, that I didn't dare try to wriggle out of it.

First of all, reducing Montaigne to brief extracts went completely against everything I had learned, and against the conventional wisdom of my student years. Back then, they were denouncing the practice of pulling traditional morals out of the *Essays* in the form of single sentences, and advocating going back to the text, with all its complexity and contradictions. Anyone trying to serve Montaigne up in bite-size pieces would have been ridiculed straight away, declared *minus habens*, and consigned to the dustbin of history like Pierre Charron, the author of *Traité de la Sagesse* (*On Wisdom*), a collection of maxims borrowed from the *Essays*. Breaking this taboo, or finding a way around it, was a tempting proposition.

Next, choosing forty or so passages of a few lines each in order to chat briefly about them, while at the same time showing both their historic significance *and* their current relevance seemed an impossibly tall order. Should I just choose pages at random, like Saint Augustine opening the Bible? Should I have a third party pick them? Should I just tear through the major themes of the book? Give a broad overview of its richness and diversity? Or should I simply focus on a few of my favorite excerpts, without worrying too much about unity or completeness? In the end I did all of these things at once, without order or premeditation.

Finally, being on the air during the time slot once occupied by Lucien Jeunesse, to whom I owe the best part of my adolescent knowledge, was an offer impossible to refuse.[1]

---

[1] Translator's note: The text referred to throughout is the 1877 edition of Charles Cotton's translation of the *Essays*, edited by William Carew Hazlitt.

# 1
## ENGAGEMENT

Because Montaigne deliberately portrayed himself as a plain-dealing man of leisure, one of the idle rich who kept himself secluded on the family estate and had withdrawn to the refuge of his library, we forget that he was also a public man deeply engaged in the affairs of the century in which he lived, and that he held significant political responsibilities during a troubled period in our history. He served as a negotiator between Catholics and Protestants, between King Henry III and Henry of Navarre, the future Henry IV, a role from which he drew this lesson:

"In the little I have had to mediate betwixt our princes in the divisions and subdivisions by which we are at this time torn to pieces, I have been very careful that they should neither be deceived in me nor deceive others by me. People of that kind of trading are very reserved, and pretend to be the most moderate imaginable and nearest to the opinions of those with whom they have to do; I expose myself in my stiff opinion, and after a method the most my own; a tender negotiator, a novice, who had rather fail in the affair than be wanting to myself. And yet it has been hitherto with so good luck (for fortune has doubtless the best share in it), that few things have passed from hand to hand with less suspicion or more favor and privacy. I have a free and open way that easily insinuates itself and obtains belief with those with whom I am to deal at the first meeting. Sincerity and pure truth, in what age soever, pass for current." (III, 1)

His entire adult life was marked by civil wars—the very worst kind of wars, he reminds us readily, because they pit friends and brothers against one another. The decades between 1562—when he was not yet thirty years old—and his death in 1592 consisted of a series of battles, skirmishes, sieges, and assassinations relieved only by brief truces.

How did he survive it all? He often wonders this in the *Essays*; this particular passage above is from the chapter entitled "Of Profit and Honesty," which opens Volume Three, written after his harrowing experience as mayor of Bordeaux during a time of war and plague.

Profit and honesty: Montaigne addresses the question of public morality, or ends and means, the reasons of state. Machiavelli and political realism were the order of the day, incarnated in the person of Catherine de' Medici, the daughter of Lorenzo II, to whom Machiavelli had dedicated *The Prince*. The Queen Mother, widow of Henry II and mother of the last three Valois kings, had given the order that unleashed the worst atrocity of the era: the Saint Bartholomew's Day massacre.

Machiavellianism asserts that it is permissible to lie, to break one's word, even to kill when it is in the best interests of the State, in order to ensure governmental stability, which is seen as the supreme good. Montaigne never became comfortable with this, denouncing dishonesty and hypocrisy wherever he found them. He invariably presents himself just as he is and says precisely what he thinks, disregarding etiquette. He prefers openness, directness, and loyalty to what he calls "the covered path." For him, the end does not justify the means, and he is never prepared to sacrifice private morality for reasons of State.

Such foolish behavior, Montaigne realizes, has done him no harm—has, in fact, brought him success. His conduct is not just more honest; it is more profitable as well. If a public figure lies once he is never believed again; he has chosen an expedient over the long term, and he has made the wrong decision.

According to Montaigne, sincerity and fidelity to one's pledged word constitute a much more profitable way of behaving. If you are not driven to honesty by moral conviction, practical reason should be incitement enough.

# 2
## CONVERSATION

How does Montaigne comport himself in conversation, whether an informal chat or an official discussion? He answers this question in the chapter "Of the Art of Conference" in Book Three of the *Essays*. Conference is dialogue, deliberation. Montaigne presents himself as a man amenable to hearing other people's ideas; open and accessible, rather than stubborn, narrow-minded, and unyielding in his opinions.

"I hail and caress truth in what quarter soever I find it, and cheerfully surrender myself, and open my conquered arms as far off as I can discover it; and, provided it be not too imperiously, take a pleasure in being reproved, and accommodate myself to my accusers, very often more by reason of civility than amendment, loving to gratify and nourish the liberty of admonition by my facility of submitting to it." (III, 8)

Montaigne assures us that he respects the truth, even when it is spoken by someone unlikeable. He is not arrogant, and does not see contradiction as a humiliation. If wrong, he prefers to be corrected. What he does *not* like in his conversational partners is conceit; people who are overly sure of themselves or intolerant.

Montaigne seems, then, to be the perfect enlightened gentleman: liberal, respectful of others' ideas, without ego; never seeking to have the last word. In short, he does not see conversation as a battle to be won.

Soon enough, however, he does add a qualification: if he does concede to an opponent, it is out of politeness more than a desire to improve himself, especially if his sparring partner is self-important. In these cases, he yields, but without altering his private convictions. Isn't this a falsehood on his part, despite his endless exaltation of sincerity? He tends to give way to his bolder adversaries, and even to others, without resisting, out of sheer courtesy—so that they can continue to disabuse and enlighten him, he says. We must cede our arms to the other, or at least let him *believe* we have done so, so that he will not hesitate to give us his opinion in the future.

"Nevertheless," Montaigne continues, "it is hard to bring the men of my time to it: they have not the courage to correct, because they have not the courage to suffer themselves to be corrected; and speak always with dissimulation in the presence of one another: I take so great a pleasure in being judged and known, that it is almost indifferent to me in which of the two forms I am so: my imagination so often contradicts and condemns itself, that 'tis all one to me if another do it, especially considering that I give his reprehension no greater authority than I choose; but I break with him, who carries himself so high, as I know of one who repents his advice, if not believed, and takes it for an affront if it be not immediately followed."

Montaigne regrets that his contemporaries do not argue

with him more, out of an aversion to being argued with themselves. Because they do not like to be contradicted, because it humiliates them, they refrain from contradicting others, and become more firmly entrenched in their own certainties.

One final point: if Montaigne gives in easily to others, it is not only out of courtesy and to encourage his conversational partners to speak freely to him; it is also because he is not always sure of himself. His opinions are changeable, and he sometimes disagrees with himself. Montaigne loves argument, but he does not need anyone else to provide it. What he detests above all are people who are so arrogant that they take offense when someone else contradicts them. If there is one thing Montaigne loathes, it is smugness, conceit.

## 3
## EVERYTHING CHANGES

Scattered throughout the *Essays* are remarks on instability, the changeability of things in this world, and man's inability to understand this. But nowhere are Montaigne's views on change so clear as here, in the opening paragraph of the chapter "Of Repentance" in Book Three. Here, Montaigne summarizes the wisdom he has earned and which has enabled him to write his book, and introduces the paradox of stability in changeability.

"Others form man; I only report him: and represent a particular one, ill fashioned enough, and whom, if I had to model him anew, I should certainly make something else than what he is but that's past recalling. Now, though the features of my picture alter and change, 'tis not, however, unlike: the world eternally turns round; all things therein are incessantly moving, the earth, the rocks of Caucasus, and the pyramids of Egypt, both by the public motion and their own. Even constancy itself is no other but a slower and more languishing motion. I cannot fix my object; 'tis always tottering and reeling by a natural giddiness; I take it as it is at the instant I consider it." (III, 2)

Montaigne begins, as he often does, by professing his own humility. His intentions are modest; he does not claim to be teaching a doctrine, unlike almost all other authors, who wish to mold and instruct. He is simply telling his own story, as a human—and, in fact, he presents himself as the polar opposite of an ideal man; he is "ill fashioned enough," and it is too late to change. He should not, he says, be taken as an example.

And yet, he seeks truth—but it is impossible to find it in such an unstable, turbulent world. Everything flows, as Heraclitus said. There is nothing solid on the earth; not the mountains or the pyramids, nor the wonders of nature, nor the monuments built by man. The object moves, and the subject does as well. How can we ever have a solid and reliable understanding of it all?

Montaigne does not deny the truth, but he doubts that it is accessible to man alone. Famously skeptical, he chose as his motto *"Que sais-je?"* ("What do I know?"), and as his emblem, a set of scales. But ignorance is no reason for despair.

"I do not paint its being," he continues, "I paint its passage; not a passing from one age to another, or, as the people say, from seven to seven years, but from day to day, from minute to minute, I must accommodate my history to the hour: I may presently change, not only by fortune, but also by intention. 'Tis a counterpart of various and changeable accidents, and of irresolute imaginations, and, as it falls out, sometimes contrary: whether it be that I am then another self, or that I take subjects by other circumstances and considerations."

In the end it is about resigning ourselves to the human condition, accepting our own misfortune. Life is about *becoming*, rather than *being*. The world can change in an instant, and so can I. In the *Essays*, an account of his thoughts and experiences, Montaigne makes a point of noting how much, and how often, everything changes. He is a relativist; one might even say a *perspectivist*: at any given moment, I have a different point of view on the world. My identity is changeable. Montaigne never found a "fixed point," but neither did he ever stop searching for one.

The best image for his relationship to the world might be that of horseback riding; of the mount upon which the knight keeps his balance, his precarious seat. *Seat*—that is the key word. The world moves, and I move; it is up to me to find my seat in the world.

# 4
## The Indians of Rouen

In 1562 in Rouen, Montaigne met three Indians from France Antarctique, the French colony in the Guanabara Bay in Rio de Janeiro. They were presented to King Charles IX, then aged twelve, who had expressed curiosity about these people indigenous to the New World. Montaigne then had a conversation with them.

"Three of these people, not foreseeing how dear their knowledge of the corruptions of this part of the world will one day cost their happiness and repose, and that the effect of this commerce will be their ruin, as I presuppose it is in a very fair way (miserable men to suffer themselves to be deluded with desire of novelty and to have left the serenity of their own heaven to come so far to gaze at ours!), were at Rouen at the time that the late King Charles IX was there. The king himself talked to them a good while, and they were made to see our fashions, our pomp, and the form of a great city." (I, 30)

Montaigne is a pessimist. Coming into contact with the Old World will cause the New World, once young and innocent, to break down; it has even happened already. The paragraph above falls at the end of "Of Cannibals." Montaigne has just depicted Brazil as a land from some golden age, like the mythical Atlantis. The Indians are primitive, not in the sense of cruelty but because they are natural and untamed—and it is we who are barbarous. If they eat their enemies it is not to feed themselves, but to obey a code of honor. In short, Montaigne forgives them for everything—and us for nothing.

"After which," he continues, "some one asked their opinion, and would know of them, what of all the things they had seen, they found most to be admired? To which they made answer, three things, of which I have forgotten the third, and am troubled at it, but two I yet remember. They said, that in the first place they thought it very strange that so many tall men, wearing beards, strong, and well armed, who were about the king ('tis like they meant the Swiss of the guard), should submit to obey a child, and that they did not rather choose out one amongst themselves to command."

In the type of inversion that Montesquieu's *Lettres persanes* (*Persian Letters*) would later popularize, it is now the Indians' turn to observe us; to wonder at our customs and note their absurdity. The first of these is "voluntary servitude," as discussed by Montaigne's friend Étienne de La Boétie. How is it possible that so many strong, grown men willingly obey a child? By what magic are they made to submit? According to La Boétie, the prince would fall from power if his people simply ceased to obey. Gandhi would later promote passive resistance and civil disobedience in these same terms. The Indian will not go so far as that, but he finds the divine right of the Old World inexplicable.

"Secondly [ . . . ] that they had observed that there

were amongst us men full and crammed with all manner of commodities, whilst, in the meantime, their halves were begging at their doors, lean and half-starved with hunger and poverty; and they thought it strange that these necessitous halves were able to suffer so great an inequality and injustice, and that they did not take the others by the throats, or set fire to their houses."

The second outrage is the inequality that exists between the rich and the poor. Montaigne paints the Indians as, if not communists *avant la lettre*, at least disciples of justice and equality.

Strangely, Montaigne fails to give us a third reason for his Indians' indignation. What could reasonably be expected to follow one political wonder and a second social one? We will never know for certain, but I have always had my own guess on the subject, which I will share some other time.

# 5
## A Fall from a Horse

This is one of the most moving passages in the *Essays*; it is rare for Montaigne to talk about an event in his life, a private moment, in such detail. The story is about a fall from a horse, and the loss of consciousness that followed.

"In the time of our third or second troubles (I do not well remember which), going one day abroad to take the air, about a league from my own house, which is seated in the very center of all the bustle and mischief of the late civil wars in France; thinking myself in all security and so near to my retreat that I stood in need of no better equipage, I had taken a horse that went very easy upon his pace, but was not very strong. Being upon my return home, a sudden occasion falling out to make use of this horse in a kind of service that he was not accustomed to, one of my train, a lusty, tall fellow, mounted upon a strong German horse, that had a very ill mouth, fresh and vigorous, to play the brave and set on ahead of his fellows, comes thundering full speed in the very track where I was, rushing like a Colossus upon the little man and the little horse, with such a career of strength and weight, that he turned us both over and over, topsy-turvy with our heels in the air: so that there lay the horse overthrown and stunned with the fall, and I ten or twelve paces from him stretched out at length, with my face all battered and broken, my sword which I had had in my hand, above ten paces beyond that, and my belt broken all to pieces, without motion or sense any more than a stock." (II, 6)

Montaigne normally speaks about his readings and the ideas they inspire him, and depicts himself in broad strokes rather than recounting stories from his own life, but here he touches upon a personal event. The narration is rich in detail; the circumstances are precisely given: this happened during the second or third civil war, between 1567 and 1570. During a brief respite, Montaigne has left his home for a leisurely ramble astride a gentle mount, with only a few companions and without leaving his own property.

Then comes the lengthy and vivid paragraph describing the misadventure, full of picturesque observations: the powerful charger ridden by one of his men; himself, "the little man and the little horse," knocked over by the enormous animal bearing down suddenly on them. We can imagine the scene clearly; we are in the Dordogne countryside amid the vines, the small group frolicking in the sun. Then, the shock: Montaigne lying on the ground, his belt and sword broken and scattered, his face bruised and bloodied. Worst of all, he has been knocked unconscious.

It is all there. Though Montaigne gives us so many details, he remembers nothing of it; one of his men has told him what happened, carefully concealing the role of the charger and its rider. What fascinates and troubles him is his loss of consciousness, and then his slow return to life after being taken for dead and carried home. The accident is the closest Montaigne has ever come to death, and the experience was a gentle, ephemeral one. Death, it appears, is nothing much to be afraid of.

Besides this moral, Montaigne learns a more important, more modern lesson from the incident. It causes him to reflect on identity, on the relationship between the mind and the body. Though unconscious, it seems that he moved, spoke, and even gave orders to look after his wife, who had been notified of the accident and ran out to meet the returning party. What are we, if our bodies move and we can talk and give directions without our will being involved? Where does the *self* exist? Thanks to a fall from a horse, Montaigne—before Descartes, before phenomenology, before Freud—anticipates by several centuries the tendency to wonder uneasily about subjectivity and intention, and conceives his own theory of identity; it is precarious, disjointed. Anyone who has fallen off a horse will understand what he means.

# 6
## THE BALANCE

Montaigne was a magistrate; he had been trained in the law and was highly attuned to the ambiguity of texts—all of them, not only law texts, but also literature, philosophy, theology. All are subject to interpretation and debate, which, rather than bringing us closer to their meaning, take us ever further away. Between them and us lie ever-multiplying layers of commentary that make their truth more and more inaccessible. Montaigne reminds us of this in "Apology for Raimond Sebond":

"Our speaking has its failings and defects, as well as all the rest. Most of the occasions of disturbance in the world are grammatical ones; our suits only spring from disputes as to the interpretation of laws; and most wars proceed from the inability of ministers clearly to express the conventions and treaties of amity of princes. How many quarrels, and of how great importance, has the doubt of the meaning of this syllable, *hoc*, created in the world?" (II, 12)

As a man of the Renaissance, Montaigne comments ironically on the medieval tradition, with its accumulation of commentaries—compared to excrement by Rabelais (*faeces literarum*)—and pleads for a return to the original texts of Plato, Plutarch, and Seneca.

But there is more. In his eyes, all of the world's troubles—trials and wars, public and private lawsuits—have to do with misunderstandings about the meaning of words, up to and including the conflict between Catholics and Protestants. Montaigne blames this on a dispute over the meaning of the syllable *Hoc* in the sacrament of the Eucharist: *Hoc est enim corpus meum, Hoc est enim calix sanguinis mei*, Christ said, and the priest repeats: "This is my body, this is my blood." According to the doctrine of transubstantiation, or the Real Presence, the bread and wine become the flesh of Christ. Calvinists, however, assert merely that Christ is spiritually present in the bread and wine. What did Montaigne, who reduces the Reformation to a quarrel over words, believe? We do not know. He kept his private convictions to himself.

"Let us take the clearest conclusion that logic itself presents us withal; if you say, 'It is fine weather,' and that you say true, it is then fine weather. Is not this a very certain form of speaking? And yet it will deceive us; that it will do so, let us follow the example: If you say, 'I lie,' if you say true, you do lie. The art, the reason, and force of the conclusion of this, are the same with the other, and yet we are gravelled."

The example of the Eucharist serves to confirm his skepticism by reiterating the paradox of the Cretan, or the liar: "A Cretan declares, 'All Cretans are liars.' If this is true, he is lying. If this is a lie, he is telling the truth." Montaigne was a disciple of Pyrrho, a Greek philosopher who advocated "suspension of judgment" as the only logical outcome of doubt. Yet, even more radically, he finds fault with the very words "I doubt," because if I say that I doubt, then of that statement itself I do not doubt. "The Pyrrhonian philosophers, I see, cannot express their general conception in any kind of speaking; for they would require a new language on purpose."

Montaigne has discovered this new language by formulating his own motto as a question rather than an affirmation: "This fancy will be more certainly understood by interrogation: 'What do I know?' as I bear it with the emblem of a balance." The balance in equilibrium represents his perplexity; his refusal, or inability, to choose.

# 7

# A HERMAPHRODITE

On the road from Germany while traveling to Rome in 1580, Montaigne met a man who had been born female and remained so for more than twenty years before becoming male:

"Myself passing by Vitry le Francois, saw a man the Bishop of Soissons had, in confirmation, called Germain, whom all the inhabitants of the place had known to be a girl till two-and-twenty years of age, called Mary. He was, at the time of my being there, very full of beard, old, and not married. He told us, that by straining himself in a leap his male organs came out; and the girls of that place have, to this day, a song, wherein they advise one another not to take too great strides, for fear of being turned into men, as Mary Germain was. It is no wonder if this sort of accident frequently happen; for if imagination have any power in such things, it is so continually and vigorously bent upon this subject, that to the end it may not so often relapse into the same thought and violence of desire, it were better, once for all, to give these young wenches the things they long for." (I, 20)

Like his contemporaries, Montaigne was fascinated by these "Memorable Stories of Certain Women who Changed into Men," the title of a chapter of *Des monstres et prodigies* (*Of Monsters and Prodigies*) by the physician Ambroise Paré. Renaissance culture was attracted by curiosities of nature such as hermaphrodites, who were both male and female at once. Mary became Germain following a physical effort that dislodged his male genitalia, which had previously been inverted, and therefore so difficult to see that people had always thought him a woman.

But Montaigne downplays the wonder of this incident. Such accidents are common; in fact, as he notes, girls are advised to avoid taking overly large strides, which might transform them into men. The cause of this is "the force of imagination," which is also the title of the chapter in which the anecdote above is found. In thinking so much about sex, young women have acted in such a way as to produce it in themselves. Their thoughts cause it to develop in them. This is not the "penis envy," put forth by Freud as a stage in every little girl's development, but feminine desire, as mysterious to Montaigne as it was to Rabelais in his *Tiers Livre*, or *The Third Book*. If you lust too greatly after men, you will become one. In this, as is so often the case, it is difficult to tell whether Montaigne is joking.

However, he moves on quickly enough, and dwells at much greater length on numerous cases of a far more ordinary situation illustrating the force of imagination: specifically, male impotence, and the "*nouement d'aiguillette,*" as a particular evil charm was known. This consisted of tying a knot in a cord while speaking a magical phrase, which would render a man impotent and prevent him from consummating his marriage. Montaigne unflinchingly begins by recounting a situation in which "a particular friend of mine," as he cheerily asserts, "one for whom I can be as responsible as for myself," came up lacking after a friend had related a failure of his own, which he thought about at precisely the wrong moment.

There can be no better illustration of the complicated relationship between mind and body than this male organ which does not respond to my orders and does only what it wishes to, as if it had its own will, independent of me, disobedient, dissolute, and rebellious: "Does she always will what we would have her to do?" Montaigne asks, representing identity as a bit of psychological theatre in which dialogues and disputes among the mind, the will, and the imagination are played out like a scene in a comedy.

# 8
## THE LOST TOOTH

Death is one of the major subjects on which Montaigne ruminates, and to which he returns again and again. The *Essays* are also a sort of preparation for death, from the chapter "That to Study Philosophy is to Learn to Die" early in Book One to the end of Book Three and its final two chapters, "Of Physiognomy," in which Montaigne praises the stoic attitude of peasants, who are exposed to the ravages of war and plague and yet remain as composed and tranquil as Socrates on the verge of drinking hemlock, to "Of Experience."

"God is favorable to those whom He makes to die by degrees; 'tis the only benefit of old age; the last death will be so much the less painful; it will kill but a half or a quarter of a man. There is one tooth lately fallen out without drawing and without pain; it was the natural term of its duration; in that part of my being and several others, are already dead, others half dead, of those that were most active and in the first rank during my vigorous years; 'tis so I melt and steal away from myself." (III, 13)

We cannot try death on for size; it only comes once. However, Montaigne takes advantage of any experience that might give him a sense of what it will be like; for example, a fall from a horse (as we have seen) followed by a blackout, which he found a gentle and peaceful kind of death. Here, the loss of a tooth gives rise to a short fable about death.

There is at least one advantage to aging, which is that we do not die all at once, but little by little, bit by bit; the process is so gradual that the "last death," as he calls it, cannot be as much of a shock as a death that happens during the bloom of youth. The loss of a tooth—a commonplace annoyance, hardly catastrophic, and one that Montaigne must have experienced—becomes a sign of aging and a harbinger of death. He compares it to other weaknesses affecting his body, including a lessening of his sex drive. Teeth and genitals: centuries before Freud, Montaigne associates them with potency—or the lack thereof, when they do not respond on cue.

"What a folly it would be in my understanding to apprehend the height of this fall, already so much advanced, as if it were from the very top! I hope I shall not." The end of the passage, though, is ambiguous: surely it would be foolish to feel the last death, which merely takes away what remains of a man, as if it were a whole death. Montaigne hopes he will not. But is he convinced of this? He is wondering it about himself, and asking the question means recognizing that there is a question to be asked. Even though he has lost a tooth and noticed other failings in his body, the final death might still be felt as deeply as if it were whole.

"Death mixes and confounds itself throughout with life; decay anticipates its hour, and shoulders itself even into the course of our advance. I have portraits of myself taken at five-and-twenty and five-and-thirty years of age. I compare them with that lately drawn: how many times is it no longer me; how much more is my present image unlike the former, than unlike my dying one?"

Here, Montaigne is rationalizing: his mind is attempting to reason with his imagination. We have photos of ourselves at various stages of life; we know that we are not the images in these yellowed snapshots anymore. Montaigne does not deny the difference between *me* now and the *me* of long ago. Still, though, something in me remains intact: that is "no longer me," he says of an old portrait. But there is still a *me*, an intact life, and it is this *me* that will one day cease to exist.

# 9
## THE NEW WORLD

The discovery of America, followed by the first colonial expeditions, had a profound impact on European minds. Some saw it as a reason for optimism, as progress for the West, which has much to thank America for: tomatoes, tobacco, vanilla, chili peppers, and especially gold. But Montaigne expresses anxiety.

"Our world has lately discovered another (and who will assure us that it is the last of its brothers, since the Daemons, the Sybils, and we ourselves have been ignorant of this till now?), as large, well-peopled, and fruitful as this whereon we live and yet so raw and childish, that we are still teaching it its ABCs: 'tis not above fifty years since it knew neither letters, weights, measures, vestments, corn, nor vines: it was then quite naked in the mother's lap, and only lived upon what she gave it. If we rightly conclude of our end [ . . . ], that other world will only enter into the light when this of ours shall make its exit; the universe will fall into paralysis; one member will be useless, the other in vigour." (III, 6)

There are still more worlds for us to discover, suggests Montaigne, and where will all of it lead us? The New World is innocent compared to the one in which Montaigne lives;

he characterizes it by what it lacks: writing, clothing, bread, and wine. Fundamental religious questions are implicit. If they all go naked without shame, like Adam and Eve in the Garden of Eden, does this mean that they never experienced the Fall? Are they exempt from original sin?

This other world, then, must be closer to a state of nature than the Old World—and nature, Mother Nature, is always a good thing for Montaigne, who, setting it against artifice, praises it endlessly. The closer we are to nature, the better off we are; this means that the lives of the men and women of the New World were better before Christopher Columbus discovered them.

Montaigne fears the imbalance that contact between these two worlds, which are at different stages in their development, will create in the universe, his perception of which is based on the model of the human body, according to a macrocosm-microcosm analogy. The universe will become like an enormous body, standing on one healthy leg, with the other leg crippled and useless. It will be misshapen, lopsided, lame.

The author of the *Essays* does not believe in progress. His cyclical philosophy of history is modeled on human life, which moves from infancy to adulthood, from greatness to decline. The colonization of America does not bode well, for the Old World will corrupt the New:

"I am very much afraid that we have greatly precipitated its declension and ruin by our contagion; and that we have sold it opinions and our arts at a very dear rate. It was an infant world, and yet we have not whipped and subjected it to our discipline by the advantage of our natural worth and force, neither have we won it by our justice and goodness, nor subdued it by our magnanimity." (III, 6)

Contact with the Old World will accelerate the New World's advancement toward its own decay and decrepitude, but without making us young again, for history moves in only one direction, and our golden age is behind us. It is not our moral superiority that has conquered the New World, but our brute strength that has subjugated it.

Montaigne had just read the first stories of the Spanish colonists' cruelty in Mexico, and their ruthless destruction of an admirable civilization. He was one of colonialism's earliest critics.

# 10
## NIGHTMARES

Why did Montaigne start writing the *Essays* in the first place? He gives us an explanation in a brief chapter in Book One entitled "Of Idleness," in which he describes the misadventures that followed his retirement in 1571:

"When I lately retired to my own house, with a resolution, as much as possibly I could, to avoid all manner of concern in affairs, and to spend in privacy and repose the little remainder of time I have to live, I fancied I could not more oblige my mind than to suffer it at full leisure to entertain and divert itself, which I now hoped it might henceforth do, as being by time become more settled and mature; but I find—

'*Variam semper dant otia mentem,*'

'Leisure ever creates varied thought.'—Lucan, iv. 704

that, quite contrary, it is like a horse that has broke from his rider, who voluntarily runs into a much more violent career than any horseman would put him to, and creates me so many chimaeras and fantastic monsters, one upon another, without order or design, that, the better at leisure to contemplate their strangeness and absurdity, I have begun to commit them to writing, hoping in time to make it ashamed of itself." (I, 8)

Here Montaigne relates the origins of the *Essays*, after

his resignation as advisor to the Parliament of Bordeaux at the age of thirty-eight. What he hoped to do next, following the Classical model, was to withdraw to a life of studious peace, lettered leisure, *otium studiosun*, in order to find himself and to know himself better. Like Cicero, Montaigne believed that man could never really be himself in public life, in the world of society and work, but only in solitude, meditation, and reading. Prioritizing the contemplative life over the active one, he was far from being one of those modern souls who insisted that man became truly realized via activity and *negotium*, negotiation, or the renunciation of *otium*, or leisure. This modern work ethic was linked to the rise of Protestantism, and *otium*, idleness, lost its supreme value to become a synonym for laziness.

But what does Montaigne say? In solitude, instead of finding serenity, discovering his fixed point, he tells us that he experienced mental distress and anxiety—the spiritual malady of melancholy, or acedia, the depression that struck monks during their rest periods, the torpor of temptation.

Age, Montaigne thought, should have given him gravity—but no, his mind was restless and unable to concentrate, "like a horse that has broke from its rider," as he beautifully describes it, running in ever direction, becoming scattered as it never did when his duties as a magistrate kept it under control. The "chimaeras and fantastic monsters" that took possession of his imagination were nightmares that tormented him, rather than the hoped-for peace, reminiscent of the Hieronymus Bosch painting *The Temptation of Saint Anthony*.

So, he tells us, he began writing. The goal of retirement

was not to write, but to read, to reflect, to meditate. Writing was invented as a remedy; a way of calming his anxiety and taming his demons. Montaigne resolved to record the things that went through his mind, to "commit them to writing." This writing was the great register, the guestbook of check-ins and check-outs. Montaigne had decided to keep an account of his own thoughts and flights of fancy, to put them in some sort of order and take back control of himself.

In short, seeking wisdom in solitude, Montaigne instead flirted with madness. He saved himself, cured himself of his delusions and hallucinations, by writing them down. Writing the *Essays*, then, allowed him to regain mastery of his own self.

# 11
## GOOD FAITH

When he published the first two volumes of the *Essays* in 1580, Montaigne prefaced them, as was customary at the time; with an important address "To the reader":

"Reader, thou hast here an honest book; it doth at the outset forewarn thee that, in contriving the same, I have proposed to myself no other than a domestic and private end: I have had no consideration at all either to thy service or to my glory. My powers are not capable of any such design."[2]

Montaigne undoubtedly conformed largely to convention in the writing of his preface, which takes the usual form of a profession of modesty, with the author presenting himself in the best possible light to his readers. But he also toys with tradition, even breaks with it, by suggesting the great originality of his undertaking.

Straight away, at the very outset of his book, he emphasizes the essential human quality to which he will pay particular attention from the first of the *Essays* to the last: faith. Good faith. Indeed, this is the only virtue he recognizes in himself; it is vitally important in his eyes, the indispensable

---

[2] All citations in this chapter come from Montaigne's one-page Preface to Books I and II of the *Essays*.

basis for every human relationship. The word comes from the Latin *fides*, which means not only faith, but also fidelity; that is, respect for the faith given, the basis for all trust. Faith, fidelity, trust, and even confidence—all of these are one. My commitment to another person, the way you give your word, the way you commit to keeping that word.

And good faith, the *bona fides* promised by Montaigne, is the absence of malice, trickery, concealment, deceit, fraud. In short, it is honesty, loyalty, the assurance that there will be no difference between appearance and reality, between the shirt and the skin. You can trust a man—and a book—of good faith, and your trust will not be abused.

Montaigne wishes to establish a relationship of trust with his reader; this is how he has conducted himself throughout his life, in every action. The basis for a relationship of trust is the absence of convenience, of gratuitousness. Montaigne will not try to educate his readers, or exalt himself, in a book that was not intended to be read by anyone beyond his intimate circle: "I have dedicated it to the particular commodity of my kinsfolk and friends," he says, so that they will remember him after his death, and be able to visit him through his words. It is for this reason that he has presented the book in such an unadorned way:

"Had my intention been to seek the world's favour, I should surely have adorned myself with borrowed beauties: I desire therein to be viewed as I appear in mine own genuine, simple, and ordinary manner, without study and artifice: for it is myself I paint."

If decorum had permitted it, Montaigne, like the Indians

of Brazil, "would most willingly have painted myself quite fully and quite naked."

The book is presented as a self-portrait, even though that was not Montaigne's initial intention when he withdrew to his estate. He does not feature in the earliest chapters himself, but realizes, little by little, that the observation of oneself is a condition for wisdom, and the depiction of oneself is a condition of self-knowledge. The necessity of the self-portrait has been made clear to him by Socrates's instruction: "Know thyself."

But if the *Essays* have been a spiritual exercise, a sort of self-examination, intended neither for the glory of the author nor for the instruction of the reader, what was the purpose of making it public, of delivering it to its audience? Montaigne concedes this point: "Thus, reader, myself am the matter of my book: there's no reason thou shouldst employ thy leisure about so frivolous and vain a subject." He pretends to warn off the reader; he provokes him: *on your way, move along, don't waste your time reading this.* As Montaigne surely knew, there is no better way to tempt an audience.

# 12
## The Seat

Montaigne is best imagined on horseback; firstly, because that was how he travelled around his own lands and between his estate and Bordeaux, as well as elsewhere in France, to Paris, Rouen, or Blois, and even further afield (during his great journey in 1580 he travelled through Switzerland and Germany all the way to Rome). But he should also be pictured this way because he never felt more comfortable anywhere than in the saddle; it was here that he found his equilibrium, his seat:

"[ . . . ] travel is in my opinion a very profitable exercise; the soul is there continually employed in observing new and unknown things, and I do not know, as I have often said, a better school wherein to model life than by incessantly exposing to it the diversity of so many other lives, fancies, and usances, and by making it relish a perpetual variety of forms of human nature. The body is, therein, neither idle nor overwrought; and that moderate agitation puts it in breath. I can keep on horseback, tormented with the stone as I am, without alighting or being weary, eight or ten hours together" (III, 9).

First of all, traveling enables us to experience the world's diversity, and Montaigne insists that there is no better education. Traveling shows us the richness of nature, proves the relativity of customs and beliefs, and shakes up our certainties; in short, it teaches us scepticism, which was Montaigne's fundamental doctrine.

Next, Montaigne gains particular physical pleasure from riding horseback, which allies movement and stability and gives the body balance and rhythm conducive to contemplation. Riding frees us from work without encouraging idleness; it lends itself to daydreaming. Horseback riding puts Montaigne in a state of "moderate agitation," a lovely combination of terms he uses to designate a sort of ideal intermediary state. Aristotle both thought and taught while walking; Montaigne has his best ideas while in the saddle, an activity that even allows him to forget about his bladder and kidney stones.

However, Montaigne also admits—as is his wont—that his taste for travel, particularly on horseback, could also be interpreted as a mark of indecision and powerlessness:

"I know very well that, to take it by the letter, this pleasure of travelling is a testimony of uneasiness and irresolution, and, in sooth, these two are our governing and predominating qualities. Yes, I confess, I see nothing, not so much as in a dream, in a wish, whereon I could set up my rest: variety only, and the possession of diversity, can satisfy me; that is, if anything can. In traveling, it pleases me that I may stay where I like, without inconvenience, and that I have a place wherein commodiously to divert myself."

To be too fond of traveling is to prove yourself incapable of stopping, of making a decision, of settling down; it is to lack confidence, to prefer inconsistency to perseverance. In this, for Montaigne, travel is a metaphor for life. He lives like he travels—aimlessly, open to the attractions of the world: "They who run after a benefit or a hare, run not [ . . . ] and the journey of my life is carried on after the same manner."

So great is Montaigne's love of riding that if he were able to choose the manner of his death, "I think I should rather choose to die on horseback than in bed." Montaigne dreamt of dying in the saddle, off on some voyage, far from his home and family. Life and death on horseback represent his philosophy perfectly.

## 13
## THE LIBRARY

Montaigne's tower is one of the most affecting visits to a writer's home you can make in France; it is at Saint-Michel-de-Montaigne, in Dordogne, near Bergerac. The large round tower dating from the 16th century is all that remains of the chateau built by his father, Pierre Montaigne, which burned down at the end of the 19th century. Montaigne spent as much of his time in this tower as he could, retreating there to read, think, and write; the library was his refuge from domestic and civil life, from worldly strife and the century's violence.

"When at home, I a little more frequent my library, whence I overlook at once all the concerns of my family. 'Tis situated at the entrance into my house, and I thence see under me my garden, court, and base-court, and almost all parts of the building. There I turn over now one book, and then another, on various subjects, without method or design. One while I meditate, another I record and dictate, as I walk to and fro, such whimsies as these I present to you here. 'Tis in the third storey of a tower, of which the ground-room is my chapel, the second storey a chamber with a withdrawing-room and closet, where I often lie, to be more retired; and above is a great wardrobe. This formerly was the most useless part of the house. I there pass away both most of the days of my life and most of the hours of those days. In the night I am never there." (III, 3)

From this corner tower Montaigne could survey his property, overseeing from afar the activities of his household—but above all he went there to find himself, to "be more retired," as he phrases it, in the "comfort" of his books. The library is famous for the many Greek and Latin phrases he had inscribed on its beams after his retirement in 1571; these bear witness to the extent of his readings, both religious and secular, and to his disillusionment. A phrase on one joist, from Ecclesiastes, *Per omnia vanitas*, "All is vanity," combining the Biblical lesson with the wisdom of Greek philosophy as it does, perhaps best summarizes his view of life.

Even more touching is his manner of presenting his activities as if they counted for nothing: leafing through a book rather than reading; dictating his daydreams rather than writing; none of it with any real aim or cohesion among the ideas. We are told, these days, that linear, prolonged, continuous reading—the kind we first learned to do—is disappearing with the advent of the digital world, but Montaigne, even then, was already—or still—championing versatile, fragmented, distracted reading, capricious and impulsive, jumping haphazardly from one book to another, taking the nuggets of wisdom wherever he found them, without worrying too much about the specific sources from which he gleaned the material for his own book. This, Montaigne insists, was the product of reverie rather than calculation.

A feeling of deep happiness suffuses the moments of studious leisure Montaigne spent in his library. Only one thing could have made it more perfect: a terrace where he could have walked while he thought—but he recoiled at the expense of building one.

"[ . . . ] and were I not more afraid of the trouble than the expense—the trouble that frights me from all business—I could very easily adjoin on either side, and on the same floor, a gallery of a hundred paces long and twelve broad, having found walls already raised for some other design to the requisite height. Every place of retirement requires a walk: my thoughts sleep if I sit still: my fancy does not go by itself, as when my legs move it: and all those who study without a book are in the same condition."

Here again, Montaigne returns to the idea that we do our best thinking when in motion.

# 14
## TO HIS FEMALE READERS

Montaigne chose to write the *Essays* in French, a decision that was anything but straightforward in the 1570s. It was only later, in 1588, that he provided an explanation for this, in the chapter "Of vanity":

"I write my book for few men and for few years. Had it been a matter of duration, I should have put it into firmer language. According to the continual variation that ours has been subject to, up to this day, who can expect that its present form should be in use fifty years hence? It slips every day through our fingers, and since I was born, it is altered above one-half. We say that it is now perfect; and every age says the same of its own." (III, 9)

Montaigne rejected Latin, the language of scholars, of philosophy and theology, in favor of the vernacular, the language of everyday life. However, renouncing the monumental language of Antiquity meant publishing his reflections in a tongue that was unstable, changeable, and perishable—and that might soon become unreadable.

This act does not seem to be rooted in false modesty; I have no pretensions, Montaigne is saying. I am not writing for the centuries to come, but for the people around me now. The excuse is not a conventional one, for Montaigne has watched his own language change during the course of his own lifetime; he has experienced its mutability himself. He warns us that the words he has used to express himself may soon become unrecognizable. Stendhal, who bet in 1830 that his work would still be read in 1880 and 1930, a half-century and even a full century after publication, placed his hopes for posterity on the permanence of the French language. Montaigne does no such thing in the *Essays*; he is speaking seriously when he concludes that the extent to which French has changed during his own life suggests the improbability of its being read much longer. Happily, he was wrong on that point.

Yet, it would have been all the easier for him to write in Latin, since he had learned that language from earliest childhood, and it was, for all intents and purposes, his mother tongue. His father had wanted him to speak Latin with perfect fluency:

"[ . . . ] the expedient my father found out for this was, that in my infancy, and before I began to speak, he committed me to the care of a German, who since died a famous physician in France, totally ignorant of our language, and very fluent and a great critic in Latin. [ . . . ] As to the rest of his household, it was an inviolable rule, that neither himself, nor my mother, nor valet, nor chambermaid, should speak anything in my company, but such Latin words as each one had learned to gabble with me." (I, 25)

If Montaigne, who spoke Latin before he spoke French, writes in French here, it is because that is the language of the readers he desires to reach. The language in which he writes is the language of the reader for whom he is writing.

In "Upon Some Verses of Virgil," addressing the daring subject of his waning sex drive, Montaigne evokes his readers—more specifically, the female ones, who will read him in secret:

"I am vexed that my *Essays* only serve the ladies for a common piece of furniture, and a piece for the hall; this chapter will make me part of the water-closet. I love to traffic with them a little in private; public conversation is without favour and without savour." (III, 5)

If Montaigne has decided to write in French, it is because his desired readers are women, who are less familiar with ancient languages than men.

You might argue that he scatters his book plentifully with quotes from the Latin poets, especially in "Upon Some Verses of Virgil," when conveying the most private information about himself, and this is true. Montaigne is no stranger to contradiction.

# 15
## WAR AND PEACE

Much of the writing in the *Essays* paints a picture of daily life in times of war—civil war, the worst kind—in which we are never sure if we will wake up tomorrow as free men, and we are obliged to leave our fate in the hands of chance, counting on luck for our survival. Thus, in the chapter "Of Vanity":

"I have a thousand times gone to bed in my own house with an apprehension that I should be betrayed and murdered that very night; compounding with fortune, that it might be without terror and with quick despatch; and, after my Paternoster, I have cried out,

*'Impius haec tam culta novalia miles habebit!'*

'Shall impious soldiers have these new-ploughed grounds?'—Virgil, Ecl., i. 71." (III, 9)

Before falling asleep, Montaigne entrusts his fate jointly to the pagan god of Fortune and our Father the Christian God—not forgetting to cite Virgil as a means of bringing them together. He knows that he cannot control his own destiny, and that he cannot ensure the safety of his own house. Yet, he realizes, we can get used to war, as we can to anything else:

"What remedy? 'tis the place of my birth, and that of

most of my ancestors; they have here fixed their affection and name. We inure ourselves to whatever we are accustomed to; and in so miserable a condition as ours is, custom is a great bounty of nature, which benumbs out senses to the sufferance of many evils. A civil war has this with it worse than other wars have, to make us stand sentinels in our own houses. [ . . . ] 'Tis a grievous extremity for a man to be jostled even in his own house and domestic repose. The country where I live is always the first in arms and the last that lays them down, and where there is never an absolute peace."

Montaigne returns often to the feeling of insecurity he experiences even in his own home, in the fragile shelter of his residence, as well as to the way in which we become accustomed to living in a state of uncertainty. This depiction of war as "ordinary" appears throughout the *Essays*; not in the sense that the battles themselves are ordinary, but the rest of it—the business of everyday life, of carrying on as usual, for example in the case of peasants, who are as calm when confronting the ravages of war as they are when facing the threat of plague.

Many of the brief early chapters in the *Essays* deal with the art of war, such as "Whether the Governor Himself Go Out to Parley" (I, 5) and "That the Hour of Parley is Dangerous" (I, 6), but as the book advances we see that it is full of small touches describing the ethics of going about one's daily life in times of war. How should we act with friends, and with enemies? How can we remain honest in the most threatening circumstances? How can we remain true to ourselves when the world around us is in a constant state of upheaval? How can freedom of movement be preserved? The *Essays* are strewn with pieces of advice, summed up in the marvelous remark: "All my little prudence in the civil wars wherein we are now engaged is employed that they may not hinder my liberty of going and coming" (III, 13), which is found in "Of Experience," the final chapter of Book Three. Montaigne's freedom of movement must be preserved because, for him, there is no asset greater than liberty.

Thus, the *Essays* offer us lessons in the art, not just of war or peace, but of peace in wartime, and a peaceful life amidst the worst kind of war.

# 16
## FRIENDS

The most significant relationship in Montaigne's life was his friendship with Étienne de la Boétie, which began in 1558, when the two men first met, and lasted until La Boétie's death in 1563. A few years of closeness, and then a loss from which Montaigne never recovered. He would recount his friend's final agony in a long and moving letter to his father. Later, the first book of the *Essays* was conceived as a tribute to his vanished comrade, whose *Discourse on Voluntary Servitude* was intended to occupy the middle of the volume, the "fairest place," while the pages written by Montaigne would have been nothing but "grotesques," decorative paintings serving merely to enhance the masterpiece (I, 27). He would give up this plan only when La Boétie's work, an argument for liberty in the face of tyranny, had been published in the form of a Protestant pamphlet. Montaigne then inserted a panegyric to friendship in its place, in the great tradition of Aristotle, Cicero, and Plutarch.

"[ ... ] what we commonly call friends and friendships, are nothing but acquaintance and familiarities, either occasionally contracted, or upon some design, by means of which there happens some little intercourse betwixt our souls. But in the friendship I speak of, they mix and work themselves into one piece, with so universal a mixture, that there is no more sign of the seam by which they were first conjoined. If a man should importune me to give a reason why I loved him, I find it could no otherwise be expressed, than by making answer: because it was he, because it was I." (I, 27)

Here, Montaigne compares friendship, in its temperance and constancy, to the love of women, which is feverish and fleeting; he also distinguishes it from marriage, which he likens to being part of a market, constraining freedom and equality as it does. This wariness with regard to women would recur in "Of Three Commerces," in which he compares love and friendship to reading. Friendship, for Montaigne, is the only truly free bond between two individuals, a relationship inconceivable under a dictatorship. It is a sublime feeling—not ordinary friendship, perhaps, but the ideal friendship that unites two souls to the point that they can no longer be distinguished from one another.

Even now, Montaigne is grappling with the mystery of his friendship with La Boétie: "Because it was he, because it was I." It took him a long time to come up with this memorable phrase, which does not appear in the 1580 and 1588 editions of the *Essays*, which stop at Montaigne's observation of the enigma. He initially wrote "because it was he" in the margins of his own copy of the book, and added "because it was I" later, in a different ink. Here, he tries again to explain their deep and immediate affinity:

"There is, beyond all that I am able to say, I know not

what inexplicable and fated power that brought on this union. We sought one another long before we met, and by the characters we heard of one another, which wrought upon our affections more than, in reason, mere reports should do; I think 'twas by some secret appointment of heaven. We embraced in our names; and at our first meeting, which was accidentally at a great city entertainment, we found ourselves so mutually taken with one another, so acquainted, and so endeared betwixt ourselves, that from thenceforward nothing was so near to us as one another."

Montaigne and La Boétie were predestined for one another before they even met. Montaigne is undoubtedly idealizing their friendship. Later in Book One, in the chapter entitled "A Consideration upon Cicero," he is clearly thinking of La Boétie when he acknowledges that he would not have written the *Essays* if he had still had a friend to whom he could have written letters. We have La Boétie to thank for the *Essays*, in his presence as much as his absence.

Montaigne was a man of the Renaissance; a near-contemporary of Erasmus, who, drawing on a humanist faith in his fellow man, believed in the superiority of the pen to the sword and, in his *Querela pacis* (*The Complaint of Peace*), called for the laying down of weapons in favor of letters, which he believed could bring peace to the world. Montaigne cherished no such illusions; he was as skeptical about the power of letters as he was about the benefits of educating Christian princes, or the ability of a negotiator to bring about peace through his powers of persuasion. His experiences in life did not encourage him to agree with the maxim that the pen is mightier than the sword, or the toga—*Cedant arma togae*, as Cicero said in *De officiis* (*On Duties*).

Montaigne mistrusted words and rhetoric. At the end of the chapter "Of Pedantry," he compares two Greek cities: Athens, where fine speeches are held in high esteem, and Sparta, where actions are preferred to words. Montaigne places himself firmly in the Spartan camp, endorsing another of the opinions he shares with it—specifically, that individuals and societies are weakened by too much erudition:

"[ . . . ] the study of sciences more softens and untempers the courages of men than it in any way fortifies and excites them. The most potent empire that at this day appears to be in the whole world is that of the Turks, a people equally inured to the estimation of arms and the contempt of letters. I find Rome was more valiant before she grew so learned." (I, 24)

It is clear that Montaigne associates Rome's decadence with the development of the arts, sciences, and letters—that is, with the refinement of its civilization.

"The most warlike nations at this time in being are the most rude and ignorant: the Scythians, the Parthians, Tamerlane, serve for sufficient proof of this. When the Goths overran Greece, the only thing that preserved all the libraries from the fire was, that someone possessed them with an opinion that they were to leave this kind of furniture entire to the enemy, as being most proper to divert them from the exercise of arms, and to fix them to a lazy and sedentary life. When our King Charles VIII, almost without striking a blow, saw himself possessed of the kingdom of Naples and a considerable part of Tuscany, the nobles about him attributed this unexpected facility of conquest to this, that the princes and nobles of Italy, more studied to render themselves ingenious and learned, than vigorous and warlike."

Montaigne provides us with a whole raft of examples—the Turks, the Goths, the French under Charles VIII—showing that a nation's strength is inversely proportional to its degree of learning, and that a nation with too much knowledge runs the risk of ruin. Montaigne is no naïve humanist enthusing over a Republic of letters; he remains a man of action, sensitive to the diminishment of nations by learning. In short, he is more of a Roman than a humanist at heart, even going so far as to praise the ignorance of Roman Antiquity: "Old Rome seems to me to have been of much greater value, both for peace and war, than that learned Rome that ruined itself." (II, 12)

There will be no excessive indulgence of letters for Montaigne; only an aristocratic insistence on the superiority of arms, "the science of obeying and commanding" (I, 24). The art of peace does not rely on rhetoric, but on force, which dissuades more than it persuades.

# 18
## Why Change?

Montaigne is suspicious of innovation. He doubts that it can improve the state of the world. The *Essays* do not contain seeds of the doctrine of progress that would flourish during the Age of Enlightenment. Any attempt at reform is condemned in the chapter "Of Vanity":

"Nothing presses so hard upon a state as innovation: change only gives form to injustice and tyranny. When any piece is loosened, it may be proper to stay it; one may take care that the alteration and corruption natural to all things do not carry us too far from our beginnings and principles: but to undertake to found so great a mass anew, and to change the foundations of so vast a building, is for them to do, who to make clean, efface; who reform particular defects by an universal confusion, and cure diseases by death." (III, 9)

Of course, when he speaks of "innovation" and "novelty," Montaigne is thinking above all of the Protestant Reformation and the civil wars that have followed it; he also has the discovery of America in mind, and the state of imbalance it has created in the universe, speeding it on the way to ruin. For him the Golden Age is behind us, in our "beginnings and principles," and any change is both dangerous and pointless. *A bird in the hand is worth two in the bush*, or even: *Anything that can go wrong, will go wrong.*

Trying to change the state of things means taking the risk of making them worse instead of better. Montaigne's skepticism has led him to be conservative, protective of customs and traditions that might be as arbitrary as anything else, but which are futile to abolish unless you are sure you can do better. What good can change do now? This is why Montaigne did not appreciate it when his friend La Boétie's treatise on voluntary servitude, which argued that civil disobedience would be enough to bring down a monarch, was misappropriated for use as an anti-monarchist pamphlet. Like all depressives, Montaigne tended to overestimate the "negative effects" of any reform, as we would put it today.

He is undoubtedly exaggerating by blaming change alone for the world's injustice and tyranny, but he argues with conviction that the redemption and restoration of the old ways are far preferable to innovation and radical reworking. There will be no new religion for Montaigne; quite the contrary, in fact. Once again, he uses the idea of the State as a human body, with its themes of microcosm and macrocosm, as a metaphor for society. And Montaigne is more suspicious than ever of medicine. Reformers, he says, are like doctors who simply prolong your death while claiming to heal you.

"The world is unapt to be cured; and so impatient of anything that presses it, that it thinks of nothing but disengaging itself at what price soever. We see by a thousand examples, that it ordinarily cures itself to its cost. The discharge of a present evil is no cure, if there be not a general amendment of condition."

Illness is our natural state. We must learn to live with it, without attempting to eradicate it. This is Montaigne's message to the agitators, to all the sorcerer's apprentices promising people a better tomorrow. Rejecting both the Protestant Reformation and the Catholic League, Montaigne, who is no adherent to dogmatic theology, but a jurist and politician, maintains that the stability of the State and rule of law are more important than doctrinal quarrels. This makes him a legitimist, and even an immobilist. Humanists were not yet men of the Enlightenment, and Montaigne was not a modern man.

# 19
## THE OTHER

The dialogue between Montaigne and others, like a literary game of mirrors, is one of the most original aspects of the *Essays*. Montaigne engages in self-reflection through books and comments on these books not to cast himself in a favorable light, but because he recognizes himself in them. As he observes in the chapter "Of the Education of Children," "neither have I said so much of others, but to get a better opportunity to explain myself" (I, 25).

What Montaigne means here is that other people enable him to better examine himself. If he reads and cites them, it is because they have given him a deeper understanding of himself. But this movement toward oneself is also a movement toward other people; self-knowledge is a prelude to reaching out. Having learned to understand himself thanks to other people, he realizes, he understands others better now as well, perhaps even better than they understand themselves:

"That long attention that I employ in considering myself, also fits rile to judge tolerably enough of others; and there are few things whereof I speak better and with better excuse. I happen very often more exactly to see and distinguish the qualities of my friends than they do themselves." (III, 13)

The company of others enables us to know ourselves, and self-knowledge allows us to understand other people. Montaigne, well before the modern philosophers, has grasped the dialectics of the self and the other; one must see *oneself as another*, as Paul Ricoeur said, in order to live a moral life. Montaigne's withdrawal to his estates was never intended as a rejection of other people, but rather a way of improving his ability to interact with them. His life was not made up of two separate parts, one active and the second idle; it was composed of intermittences, periods of retirement and contemplation followed by well thought-out returns to civil life and public action.

It is in this context that we are tempted to interpret this wonderful phrase from the final chapter of the *Essays*: "Speaking is half his who speaks, and half his who hears." In accordance with the complementarity between "me" and others that Montaigne often praises, words—as long as they are true—are shared between the people who speak them, and others speak through me.

However, we should be cautious in our interpretation of this lovely thought, and refrain from idealizing it. Montaigne's next words cast a less friendly and cooperative, more aggressive and competitive light on wordplay: "[ . . . ] the latter ought to prepare himself to receive it, according to its bias; as with tennis-players, he who receives the ball, shifts and prepares, according as he sees him move who strikes the stroke, and according to the stroke itself."

Montaigne is comparing conversation to a game of tennis, a confrontation in which one person wins and the other

loses, in which they are adversaries and rivals. We must not
make a mistake about this. It is not for us to make ourselves
accessible to others; it is for them to reckon with us. In the
chapter "Of the Art of Conference," Montaigne admits
that he finds it extremely difficult to admit that another
person is right. But for the exchange to be worthwhile, as
with a game of tennis, both parties must give and take.

Thus, Montaigne hovers between perceiving conversation as an exchange and as a duel. Yet it is trust that wins
the day, for example in this open-hearted phrase from the
chapter "Of Profit and Honesty": "One open way of speaking introduces another open way of speaking, and draws
out discoveries, like wine and love." (III, 1)

The *Essays* grew significantly longer from one edition to the next. Until his death, Montaigne never stopped rereading his work, adding citations and developing ideas in the margins of his book. He comments on this practice in the chapter "Of Vanity," fittingly, in a late addition to Book Three:

"My book is always the same, saving that upon every new edition (that the buyer may not go away quite empty) I take the liberty to add (as 'tis but an ill jointed marquetery) some supernumerary emblem; it is but overweight, that does not disfigure the primitive form of the essays, but, by a little artful subtlety, gives a kind of particular value to every one of those that follow." (III, 9)

Montaigne is looking back over his work. His ironic tone is clear; he speaks of his additions as if he were a shopkeeper and his customers were readers he is trying to attract by putting an ever-greater variety of items on sale, by refreshing his stock. Montaigne pokes fun at himself and his work by comparing himself to an artisan; his book is nothing more than an assemblage of parts fitted together, a mosaic of disparate pieces, a motley creation that can be added to indefinitely, whenever the opportunity arises.

"Supernumerary emblem," "little artful subtlety": the terms Montaigne uses to describe this quality of being "overweight" are ambiguous and slightly affected; concrete and abstract at the same time. Still, they bear witness to his uncertainty about the meaning and direction of his ever-expanding book, a subject to which he returns often. He adds things, he says elsewhere, but does not correct anything (II, 37). This is not quite true, but it does warn readers that they may stumble across differences and even points that clash or contradict one another. The additions are random; they stem from something new he has happened to encounter in a book or in life. But, as Montaigne makes a point of telling us, we must not take these changes as improvements or evolutions, of either himself or his work:

"[M]y understanding does not always go forward, it goes backward too. I do not much less suspect my fancies for being the second or the third, than for being the first, or present, or past; we often correct ourselves as foolishly as we do others. I am grown older by a great many years since my first publications, which were in the year 1580; but I very much doubt whether I am grown an inch the wiser. I now, and I anon, are two several persons; but whether better, I cannot determine." (III, 9)

Montaigne's skepticism is extreme. The first version of the *Essays* was not inferior; age does not increase wisdom, and the new themes in the book are no more certain than the earlier ones. The paradox is clear: "I now, and I anon, are two several [separate] persons," he insists, but "my book is always the same." This is a contradiction, to which

Montaigne freely admits: I am always changing, but I remain myself in any and all of my actions and my thoughts. He is coming, little by little, to identify himself completely with his book: "I have no more made my book than my book has made me: 'tis a book consubstantial with the author" (II, 18), and "who touches the one, touches the other" (III, 2). Man and book have become one.

# 21
## The Skin and the Shirt

Montaigne was a political man, an involved and engaged man, as I have said. However, he was always careful not to get too caught up in the game; he maintained a certain level of detachment, observing himself as if he were watching a play. He explains this in the chapter "Of Managing the Will" in Book Three of the *Essays*, discussing his service as mayor of Bordeaux:

"'Most of our business is farce':
*'Mundus universus exercet histrioniam.'*
—Petronius Arbiter, iii. 8.

We must play our part properly, but withal as a part of a borrowed personage; we must not make real essence of a mask and outward appearance; nor of a strange person, our own; we cannot distinguish the skin from the shirt: 'tis enough to meal the face, without mealing the breast." (III, 10)

The world is a theater. Montaigne is using a common theme here, familiar since Antiquity. We are actors, masks; therefore we must not mistake ourselves for the roles we play. We have to act with conscience and fulfill our responsibilities, but we must not confuse our actions with who we are. We must maintain the margin between our inner life and our worldly affairs.

Is Montaigne giving us a lesson in hypocrisy? As a teenager reading the *Essays* for the first time, I thought so, and was suspicious of this kind of subtle distinction. Young people yearn for sincerity, authenticity, and thus perfect, ideal transparency and agreement between what is and what appears to be. The adolescent Hamlet rejects courtly manners and refuses any compromise: "I know not *seems*," he cries to the queen, his mother.

Later, we discover that it is better for powerful people not to take themselves too seriously; not to identify so fully with their duties. It is better for them to keep a certain sense of humor or irony. This is what they meant in the Middle Ages, more or less, when they put forward the doctrine of the king's two bodies, the political, immortal body and the physical, mortal one. The sovereign must not confuse himself as an individual with the responsibility he holds, but neither must he doubt his own position too much, which could compromise his authority, as happened to another of Shakespeare's heroes, Richard II, who was too conscious of the fact that he was playing a role, and was soon deposed.

Montaigne prefers to do business with men who, to put it simply, are not big-headed:

"I see some who transform and transubstantiate themselves into as many new shapes and new beings as they undertake new employments; and who strut and fume even to the heart and liver, and carry their state along with them even to the close-stool: I cannot make them distinguish the salutations made to themselves from those made to their commission, their train, or their mule:

'*Tantum se fortunx permittunt, etiam ut naturam dediscant.*'

'They so much give themselves up to fortune, as even to unlearn nature.'—Quintus Curtius, iii. 2.

They swell and puff up their souls, and their natural way of speaking, according to the height of their magisterial place. The Mayor of Bordeaux and Montaigne have ever been two by very manifest separation."

Montaigne may not have "acted Important" once elected mayor, as the philosopher Alain put it, but this did not mean that he didn't exercise every prerogative of his position with decisiveness, despite what his words in this chapter might suggest. There can be no praise for hypocrisy when it requires what is to be different from what appears to be. Rather, Montaigne counsels clear-headedness and, long before Pascal, cautions us against being dishonest with ourselves.

# 22
## THE WELL-MADE HEAD

In any debate over education, someone invariably mentions Rabelais and Montaigne: Rabelais, who argued via his creations Gargantua and Pantagruel that a school should be an "abyss of knowledge," and Montaigne, who preferred a man with a "well-made head" rather than a "well-filled" one. These two concepts, laid out here in opposition to one another, are the two objectives of every pedagogical endeavor: *knowledge* on one hand, and *skills* on the other, to use modern jargon. Montaigne protested against overstuffing pupils' heads in the chapters "Of Pedantry" and "Of the Education of Children" in Book One of the *Essays*:

"In plain truth, the cares and expense our parents are at in our education, point at nothing, but to furnish our heads with knowledge; but not a word of judgment and virtue. Cry out, of one that passes by, to the people: 'O, what a learned man!' and of another, 'O, what a good man!'—[Translated from Seneca, Ep., 88.]—they will not fail to turn their eyes, and address their respect to the former. There should then be a third crier, 'O, the blockheads!' Men are apt presently to inquire, does such a one understand Greek or Latin? Is he a poet? or does he write in prose? But whether he be grown better or more discreet, which are qualities of principal concern, these are never thought of." (I, 24)

Montaigne is putting the teaching practices of his time on trial. The Renaissance claimed to have broken with the darkness of the Middle Ages and rediscovered ancient learning, but quantity of instruction continued to be favored over the quality of its assimilation. Montaigne preferred wisdom to knowledge for its own sake, denouncing the folly of an encyclopedic education in which learning became a goal in itself. Knowledge, he believed, matters less than what one does with it; that is, practical know-how and life skills. People may admire wise men, but they respect knowledgeable men. Montaigne goes on to drive his point home:

"We should rather examine, who is better learned, than who is more learned. We only labour to stuff the memory, and leave the conscience and the understanding unfurnished and void. Like birds who fly abroad to forage for grain, and bring it home in the beak, without tasting it themselves, to feed their young; so our pedants go picking knowledge here and there, out of books, and hold it at the tongue's end, only to spit it out and distribute it abroad."

I will return to Montaigne's suspicion of memory. He often apologizes for lacking a good memory, but deep down he does not mind at all, for memory is not an asset when it is used at the expense of judgment. Montaigne compares reading, and any kind of instruction, to digestion. Lessons, like food, should not only be tasted with the lips and swallowed raw, but chewed slowly, and ruminated on in the stomach, in order to nourish the body and mind with their content. Otherwise we vomit them back up, like foreign food. Education, according to Montaigne, is about acquiring knowledge; children must make this knowledge their own and integrate it into their own judgment.

The debate over the purpose of schooling has yet to be resolved. To sum up the positions, though, it would be unfair to pit Montaigne's liberalism too hastily against the encyclopedism of Rabelais. First of all, though the letter from Pantagruel to Gargantua may seem to propose exhaustive, excessive learning, we must remember that it is intended for a giant. And the letter goes on to give a piece of advice that Montaigne would not have disagreed with: "Knowledge without Conscience is but the ruin of the soul." Conscience—that is, honesty and morality—is indeed the end goal of all teaching. It is what remains when digestion is complete and we have forgotten almost every-thing else.

# 23

# AN ACCIDENTAL PHILOSOPHER

Montaigne was distrustful of education that was too scholarly, as I have just discussed. In alignment with the great polarity that marks the thinking in the *Essays*, the opposition of nature and art, of good nature and evil artifice, erudition is more likely to distance us from our own true nature than to put us closer in touch with it. Montaigne tells us with pride that his readings have not turned him away from his own nature, but, on the contrary, have enabled him to understand it.

"My manners are natural, I have not called in the assistance of any discipline to erect them; but, weak as they are, when it came into my head to lay them open to the world's view, and that to expose them to the light in a little more decent garb I went to adorn them with reasons and examples, it was a wonder to myself accidentally to find them conformable to so many philosophical discourses and examples. I never knew what regimen my life was of till it was near worn out and spent; a new figure—an unpremeditated and accidental philosopher." (II, 12)

This definition, found in "Apology for Raimond Sebond," is a superb description of Montaigne's personal ethics, at once modest and ambitious. Montaigne is telling us two essential things. The first of these is that he has made himself who he is, that his readings and the knowledge he has acquired have neither changed him nor degraded him; that his manners—that is, his character, his behaviour, his moral qualities—are his own, and not modelled on anyone else's. The second thing Montaigne's words tell us is that, when a person writes, and speaks, and talks about himself with examples and explanations—that is, giving specific cases and his reasoning in these cases—that person will begin to see himself in books. Montaigne is telling us that writing and describing himself enabled him to understand not only who he was, but the system or group or school of thought with which he identified the most. In short, Montaigne did not choose to become a Stoic, or a skeptic, or an epicurean—the three philosophies with which he is most often associated—but he has recognized now, late in life, that his behaviour conformed naturally to one or another of these doctrines, by chance, and spontaneously, without planning or deliberation.

This is why it would be wrong to explain Montaigne in terms of his belonging to this or that Classical-era philosophical school. Montaigne detests authority. If he aligns himself with an author, it is to indicate an accidental discovery, and if he refrains from mentioning the name of an author he cites, it is so that his readers will learn to be wary of any claims of authority, as he says in the chapter "Of Books":

"I do not number my borrowings, I weigh them; and had I designed to raise their value by number, I had made them twice as many; they are all, or within a very few, so famed and ancient authors, that they seem, methinks, themselves sufficiently to tell who they are, without giving me the trouble. In reasons, comparisons, and arguments, if I transplant any into my own soil, and confound them amongst my own, I purposely conceal the author. [ . . . ] I will have them give Plutarch a fillip on my nose, and rail against Seneca when they think they rail at me." (II, 10)

If Montaigne conceals the sources of some of his ideas, it is so that his readers will not be swayed by the prestige of the ancients, and so that they will feel able to challenge their authority, just as they might challenge Montaigne's own.

# 24
## A TRAGIC LESSON

During the Guyenne revolt against the salt tax after its reintroduction by King Henry II, Tristan de Moneins, a lieutenant of the King of Navarre sent to Bordeaux to restore order, was killed by rioters on August 21, 1548. Montaigne was present at this memorable event; his father, Pierre Eyquem, was then a *jurat*, or municipal magistrate, and Montaigne himself was a boy of fifteen.

"I saw, when I was a boy, a gentleman, who was governor of a great city, upon occasion of a popular commotion and fury, not knowing what other course to take, go out of a place of very great strength and security, and commit himself to the mercy of the seditious rabble, in hopes by that means to appease the tumult before it grew to a more formidable head; but it was ill for him that he did so, for he was there miserably slain." (I, 23)

It was an appalling act of butchery. Moneins was stabbed, skinned, dismembered, and then "salted like a piece of beef." According to a contemporary account, "adding mockery to cruelty, they opened the body of Moneins in several places and filled it with salt, to demonstrate that it was hatred of the salt tax that had caused them to revolt." For the young Montaigne, the shock was never to be forgotten.

However, Montaigne points out in the chapter entitled "Various Events from the Same Counsel," if Moneins was executed, it was because of his own indecisiveness in the face of the howling mob:

"[ . . . ] But I am not, nevertheless, of opinion, that he committed so great an error in going out, as men commonly reproach his memory withal, as he did in choosing a gentle and submissive way for the effecting his purpose, and in endeavouring to quiet this storm, rather by obeying than commanding, and by entreaty rather than remonstrance."

Moneins's own behaviour, Montaigne insists, was what led to his death. A ruthless clampdown followed the uprising in Bordeaux: the city was deprived of its privileges; its municipal magistrates, including Pierre Eyquem, were suspended; and Geoffroy de La Chassaigne, grandfather of Montaigne's future wife, was left destitute. The episode left a permanent impression on Montaigne, and he remembered its lessons when, as mayor of Bordeaux in his turn, he also had to face a hostile crowd—this time in May 1585, at the end of his second term in office, at a time of extreme tension between members of the Catholic League and the city's magistrates. Despite fears of an insurrection, he decided to proceed with the annual review of the armed gentry:

"It was upon a time intended that there should be a general muster of several troops in arms (and that is the most proper occasion of secret revenges, and there is no place where they can be executed with greater safety) [ . . . ].

Whereupon a consultation was held, and several counsels were proposed, as in a case that was very nice and of great difficulty; and moreover of grave consequence. Mine, amongst the rest, was, that they should by all means avoid giving any sign of suspicion, but that the officers who were most in danger should boldly go, and with cheerful and erect countenances ride boldly and confidently through the ranks [ . . . ]. This was accordingly done, and served so good use, as to please and gratify the suspected troops, and thenceforward to beget a mutual and wholesome confidence and intelligence amongst them."

Where Moneins showed hesitation, Montaigne attributes his own success to his self-assurance, to the confidence he displayed in the face of danger, and to his cheerfulness and openness. Without arrogance, he tells us how he made a difficult decision. He does not tell us outright that he remembered the tragic scene he had witnessed forty years earlier, but the fact that the second story follows immediately after the first one speaks for itself. Moments such as these, experienced with such intensity, gravity, and simplicity, are a rarity in the *Essays*.

In the chapter "Of Three Commerces" in Book Three, Montaigne compares the three types of companionship that have occupied him for most of his life: that of "beautiful and honorable women," of "rare and exquisite friendships," and finally, of books, which he deems more profitable and healthful than either of the first two attachments:

"These two engagements are fortuitous, and depending upon others; the one is troublesome by its rarity, the other withers with age, so that they could never have been sufficient for the business of my life. That of books, which is the third, is much more certain, and much more our own. It yields all other advantages to the two first, but has the constancy and facility of its service for its own share." (III, 3)

Montaigne has not had another real friend since La Boétie's death, and in the chapter "Upon Some Verses of Virgil" he laments the decline of his sex drive. These two kinds of contact undoubtedly give rise to more feverish displays of feeling, more intense sensations, because they involve interaction with other people—but they are also more fleeting and unpredictable, and more prone to interruption. Reading, however, offers the twin advantages of patience and permanence.

This parallel between love, friendship, and reading, which compose a sort of gradation, might seem shocking. We might think Montaigne is telling us that reading, which requires solitude, is superior to any relationship involving another person, which are merely diversions that take us away from ourselves. Books, then, would make better friends or lovers than real people. But before we jump to this conclusion, we should remember that Montaigne never sees life as anything but a dialectic between the self and others. Though the rarity of friendship and the fleeting nature of love may drive us to favor the refuge of books, reading will inevitably lead us toward other people. Still, of the "three commerces," we must admit that reading is the best:

"It goes side by side with me in my whole course, and everywhere is assisting me: it comforts me in old age and solitude; it eases me of a troublesome weight of idleness, and delivers me at all hours from company that I dislike: it blunts the point of griefs, if they are not extreme, and have not got an entire possession of my soul. To divert myself from a troublesome fancy, 'tis but to run to my books; they presently fix me to them and drive the other out of my thoughts, and do not mutiny at seeing that I have only recourse to them for want of other more real, natural, and lively commodities; they always receive me with the same kindness."

The companionship of books is always available. Old age, loneliness, idleness, boredom, grief, anxiety—all of these hardships we encounter in the ordinary course of life can be alleviated by reading, if our distress is not too acute. Books soothe our worries, offering aid and assistance.

Yet there is a hint of irony in this attractive portrayal of books. They never complain, or protest when they are neglected, as flesh-and-blood men and women do. The presence of books is always a kindly and serene one, while the moods of friends and lovers vary.

Poised on the brink of the modern era, Montaigne was one of those who, through his praise of reading, helped to introduce the culture of printed material. At a time when we may be on the verge of leaving it behind, it is good to remember that men and women found comfort, understanding, and familiarity in books for centuries in the western world.

Montaigne owed his understanding of sexual reproduction
to the medical science of his time, which drew on the teach-
ings of Aristotle, Hippocrates, and Galen. These men
attributed the greatest reproductive power to the genera-
tive faculties of sperm. Thus Montaigne rhapsodizes about
the mysteries of the transmission of familial characteristics
in the last chapter of Book Two of the *Essays*, "Of the
Resemblance of Children to Their Fathers":

"What a wonderful thing it is that the drop of seed
from which we are produced should carry in itself the
impression not only of the bodily form, but even of the
thoughts and inclinations of our fathers! Where can that
drop of fluid matter contain that infinite number of
forms? and how can they carry on these resemblances
with so precarious and irregular a process that the son
shall be like his great-grandfather, the nephew like his
uncle?" (II, 37)

Montaigne sees the reproduction of familial traits as
something "wonderful," incredible, and admirable. In the
Renaissance, men such as the physicians Ambroise Paré
and Rabelais took a deep interest in the process and
sought to explain it. Like them, Montaigne believes that

women play a much less important role in procreation than men:

"[ . . . ] we see women that, without knowledge of man, do sometimes of themselves bring forth inanimate and formless lumps of flesh, but [ . . . ] to cause a natural and perfect generation they are to be husbanded with another kind of seed" (I, 8). This seed is responsible not only for physical resemblance, but also aspects of character, temperament, and mood that are passed down through a line from generation to generation.

Montaigne had deeply personal reasons to wonder so passionately about the mysteries of reproduction. He believed that the painful kidney stones from which he suffered had been inherited from his father, Pierre Eyquem—a prophetic name, as *pierre* means *stone* in French:

"'Tis to be believed that I derive this infirmity from my father, for he died wonderfully tormented with a great stone in his bladder; he was never sensible of his disease till the sixty-seventh year of his age; and before that had never felt any menace or symptoms of it, either in his reins [kidneys], sides, or any other part, and had lived, till then, in a happy, vigorous state of health, little subject to infirmities, and he continued seven years after in this disease, dragging on a very painful end of life. I was born about five-and-twenty years before his disease seized him, and in the time of his most flourishing and healthful state of body, his third child in order of birth: where could his propension to this malady lie lurking all that while? And he being then so far from the infirmity, how could that small part of his substance wherewith he made me, carry away so great an impression for its share? and how so concealed, that till five-and-forty years after, I did not begin to be sensible of it? being the only one to this hour, amongst so many brothers and sisters, and all by one mother, that was ever troubled with it. He that can satisfy me in this point, I will believe him in as many other miracles as he pleases; always provided that, as their manner is, he does not give me a doctrine much more intricate and fantastic than the thing itself for current pay." (II, 37)

Montaigne cannot believe that the paternal illness from which he suffers lay dormant in him for so long before afflicting his kidneys, or that it has affected only him among all of his brothers and sisters, but—since he is deeply suspicious of doctors—he rejects in advance any outlandish explanations they might come up with for the phenomenon. Even when dealing with something as personal as his kidney stones, Montaigne never stops doubting, observing, and wondering.

Montaigne's religious beliefs remain enigmatic. The person who manages to figure out what he truly believed will be clever indeed. Was he a good Catholic, or a secret atheist? He died as a Christian, and his contemporaries were accustomed to his acts of faith, for example when he travelled to Rome in 1580. However, by the early 17th century his views were seen as precursors of libertinism, a precursor to the free thinking that would mark the Enlightenment.

He draws a clear line between faith and reason in "Apology for Raimond Sebond," the lengthy and complex theological chapter in Book Two of the *Essays*: "'Tis faith alone that lively mind certainly comprehends the deep mysteries of our religion" (II, 12), he says straightaway, while human reason—powerless, humbled, consigned to the ranks of the animals, cannot prove either the existence of God or the truth of religion. His attitude has been characterized as "fideism," a doctrine that considers faith a blessing, a gift freely given by God that has nothing to do with reason. The advantage of this faith is that it leaves reason free to examine everything else, which Montaigne does with extreme daring; so well, in fact, that he seems to retain nothing of religion but this faith, maintained to the last, despite and behind everything, as much at odds as it seems to be with the human condition. In "Apology," Montaigne casts doubt on everything only to proclaim his faith in conclusion, as if nothing else matters.

"Christian skepticism" as it is known, was—even before Pascal's wager—doubt leading to faith. But what is this faith worth if relativism has made all religions equal, and if religion is based on nothing more than tradition? We adopt the faith of our country, just as we adhere to its customs and obey its laws, but it is no more well thought out than that:

"All this is a most evident sign that we only receive our religion after our own fashion, by our own hands, and no otherwise than as other religions are received. Either we are happened in the country where it is in practice, or we reverence the antiquity of it, or the authority of the men who have maintained it, or fear the menaces it fulminates against misbelievers, or are allured by its promises. These considerations ought, 'tis true, to be applied to our belief but as subsidiaries only, for they are human obligations. Another religion, other witnesses, the like promises and threats, might, by the same way, imprint a quite contrary belief. We are Christians by the same title that we are Perigordians or Germans."

Taken literally, statements such as this one are troubling, even blasphemous: religions are handed down by means of custom and the superstitions attached to what they promise or threaten. Montaigne does suggest that other considerations, less human and more transcendent, are vital to faith—still in the fideist sense—but the loss of them is no less destructive; if we are Christians just as we are Perigordians or Germans, what remains of the truth and universality of the Catholic church? "What sort of truth can that be, which these mountains limit to us, and make a lie to all the world beyond them?" we read later in the "Apology."

And what, then, is the distinction between Catholics and Protestants? Montaigne never takes the risk of saying what he thinks of transubstantiation, the presence of the body of Christ in the bread and wine, but—God knows why—I have always thought (and I did promise to touch on this again, remember) that this was the third thing that confused the Indians he met in Rouen in 1562.

Montaigne speaks about his own sexuality with an openness that can be disconcerting today. In the chapter "Upon Some Verses of Virgil" in Book Three of the *Essays*, he mourns the lost vigor of his youth. Still, he clearly feels some need to justify himself, which proves that he has not broken a taboo without suffering any qualms.

"But let us come to my subject: what has the act of generation, so natural, so necessary, and so just, done to men, to be a thing not to be spoken of without blushing, and to be excluded from all serious and moderate discourse? We boldly pronounce kill, rob, betray, and that we dare only to do betwixt the teeth. Is it to say, the less we expend in words, we may pay so much the more in thinking? For it is certain that the words least in use, most seldom written, and best kept in, are the best and most generally known: no age, no manners, are ignorant of them, no more than the word bread they imprint themselves in every one without being expressed, without voice, and without figure; and the sex that most practises it is bound to say least of it. 'Tis an act that we have placed in the franchise of silence, from which to take it is a crime even to accuse and judge it; neither dare we reprehend it but by periphrasis and picture." (III, 5)

Montaigne wonders at length about what it is that keeps us from talking about sex, while we speak without hesitation about so many other activities that are far less natural and more reprehensible, such as betrayal, or crimes like theft and murder. This is an important reflection on a major human emotion: shame. Why do we resist speaking about what we do every day? How can we justify our prudishness when it comes to sex? Montaigne has an explanation: we think about it all the more because we talk about it less. In other words, if we rarely speak about it, it is so that we can spend more time thinking about it. We keep the words quiet but we are perfectly familiar with them, and we cherish them all the more because they remain secret. In short, the mystery surrounding sex contributes to its glamour. Montaigne is thinking particularly of women here—"the sex that most practises it" and says the least about it; in this he is echoing a misogyny that was firmly entrenched during the Renaissance, one of which Rabelais gives us numerous examples, describing women as a self-driven and voracious animal the same way that Plato and his contemporaries did.

However, Montaigne points out a major secondary benefit of the taboo that weighs so heavily on sex: since we can't talk about it openly, we find other ways of discussing it, "by periphrasis and picture"; that is, in poetry and paintings. Art is a way of sidestepping our shame and prudishness; it represents our search for a veiled, discreet, indirect way of speaking about sex.

As for misogyny, Montaigne happily renounces it at the chapter's close, strongly affirming his belief in the equality of men and women:

"I say that males and females are cast in the same mould, and that, education and usage excepted, the difference is not great. Plato indifferently invites both the one and the other to the society of all studies, exercises, and vocations, both military and civil, in his Commonwealth; and the philosopher Antisthenes rejected all distinction betwixt their virtue and ours. It is much more easy to accuse one sex than to excuse the other; 'tis according to the saying,

'*Le fourgon se moque de la paele.*'
'The Pot Calling the Kettle Black.'" (III, 5)

Montaigne is well aware that he is falling back on cliché when he caricaturizes feminine sexuality; the fireplace poker and the dustpan, obvious sexual symbols, are employed side by side, one just as ridiculous—and shameful—as the other.

## 29
## DOCTORS

Montaigne did not like doctors at all, as I have said. In fact, this might be the profession against which he rages most readily. Doctors, he insists, are incompetents or even charlatans who, in particular, have failed to cure him of his kidney stones. He passes judgment on them everywhere in the *Essays*; here is an example from the last chapter of Book Two, "Of the Resemblance of Children to Their Fathers":

"[ . . . ] for amongst all my acquaintance, I see no people so soon sick, and so long before they are well, as those who take much physic; their very health is altered and corrupted by their frequent prescriptions. Physicians are not content to deal only with the sick, but they will moreover corrupt health itself, for fear men should at any time escape their authority. Do they not, from a continual and perfect health, draw the argument of some great sickness to ensue?" (II, 37)

Montaigne is exaggerating, obviously; men and women who follow their doctor's instructions, he claims, are sicker than anyone else. Physicians prescribe remedies or diets that do more harm than good, adding the disadvantages of treatment to those of illness. They make people sick in order to ensure their power over them; doctors, Montaigne says, are sophists who twist and distort health into a symptom of illness. In short, it is better not to have anything to do with them, if you wish to remain healthy.

Medicine in Montaigne's time was crude and uncertain, and there were plenty of excellent reasons to mistrust it and avoid it. Montaigne found favor with only one medical technique: surgery, because it cut cleanly away the places where illness was clearly present, thus involving less conjecture and guesswork—"by reason that it sees and feels what it does," he observes in the same chapter—but it was extremely risky. Otherwise, Montaigne saw no great difference between medicine and magic, and in the end he felt he could rely only on himself for care, which meant following his own natural inclinations:

"I have been sick often enough, and have always found my sicknesses easy enough to be supported (though I have made trial of almost all sorts), and as short as those of any other, without their help, or without swallowing their ill-tasting doses. The health I have is full and free, without other rule or discipline than my own custom and pleasure. Every place serves me well enough to stay in, for I need no other conveniences, when I am sick, than what I must have when I am well. I never disturb myself that I have no physician, no apothecary, nor any other assistance, which I see most other sick men more afflicted at than they are with their disease. What! Do the doctors themselves show us more felicity and duration in their own lives, that may manifest to us some apparent effect of their skill?"

In the name of nature, Montaigne erases the line

between sickness and health. Illnesses are natural; they have their life cycles and spans, and it is better to submit than to try to fight them. The refusal of medical treatment is part of submitting to nature. Therefore, Montaigne changes his habits as little as possible when he is sick.

Then comes the parting shot: doctors do not have better or longer lives than the rest of us; they suffer the same illnesses and do not heal any faster. In this case, we should probably not follow Montaigne's advice too quickly. Our doctors are no longer the sorcerer's apprentices of the Renaissance, and I think we can trust them.

# 30
## The Aim and the End

There has been much debate as to whether Montaigne's thinking evolved as he was writing the *Essays*, or if it was always disordered, multifaceted, shifting. There is certainly one subject which was on his mind a great deal, and which he seems to speak about differently at the beginning and end of the book: death. One substantial chapter in the first book borrows its title from Cicero—"That to Study Philosophy is to Learn to Die"—and is apparently inspired by the most severe kind of Stoicism:

"The end of our race is death; 'tis the necessary object of our aim, which, if it fright us, how is it possible to advance a step without a fit of ague? The remedy the vulgar use is not to think on't; but from what brutish stupidity can they derive so gross a blindness? [ . . . ] Let us disarm him of his novelty and strangeness, let us converse and be familiar with him, and have nothing so frequent in our thoughts as death." (I, 19)

The wise man must learn to control his passions, including his fear of death; because death is inevitable, we must "tame" it, get used to it, think about it all the time, in order to overcome the fear that this implacable adversary causes in us.

At the end of the *Essays*, however, Montaigne seems to

have realized, by observing the resignation of peasants in the face of plague and war, that we cannot prepare ourselves for death through an act of will, and that the lack of curiosity on the part of these simple people constitutes real wisdom, as noble as that of Socrates, condemned to suicide:

"We trouble life by the care of death, and death by the care of life: the one torments, the other frights us. It is not against death that we prepare, that is too momentary a thing; a quarter of an hour's suffering, without consequence and without damage, does not deserve especial precepts: to say the truth, we prepare ourselves against the preparations of death. [ . . . ] [B]ut I fancy that, though it be the end, it is not the aim of life; 'tis its end, its extremity, but not, nevertheless, its object; it ought itself to be its own aim and design" (III, 12).

Montaigne enjoys a good play on words: death is the end (*le bout*), not the aim (*le but*) of life. Life must be aimed at living, and death will take care of itself.

But has he evolved with age? There is no clear answer. In "That to Study Philosophy is to Learn to Die," he gives advice in the form of counterarguments so sophisticated that they could cause us to doubt his private adherence to the theory they express:

"Where death waits for us is uncertain; let us look for him everywhere. The premeditation of death is the premeditation of liberty; he who has learned to die has unlearned to serve. There is nothing evil in life for him who rightly comprehends that the privation of life is no evil: to know how to die delivers us from all subjection and constraint." (I, 19)

It is as if his mind is reasoning with his imagination, but without quite managing to believe it; as if he is repeating a lesson. He even seems to comment ironically on the fight against death, which we all lose in advance: "Were it an enemy that could be avoided, I would then advise to borrow arms even of cowardice itself"—that is, to run away.

Montaigne has not truly evolved while writing the *Essays*; not even in his attitude toward death. He is still hesitant, uncertain. How can we live our best lives? By having death always on our minds, like Cicero and the Stoics, or by thinking about it as little as possible, like Socrates and the peasants? Torn between melancholy and *joie de vivre*, Montaigne, like all of us, has waffled back and forth, and his final message is an echo of what he has said since the beginning: "[L]et death take me planting my cabbages."

# 31

# Part of Himself

In the 1595 posthumous edition of the *Essays*, Montaigne closes the chapter "Of Presumption," in which he has described himself and then several notable contemporaries, by lavishly praising Marie de Gournay, his adopted daughter. Because these complimentary lines do not appear in the previous editions, and because Mademoiselle de Gournay herself edited this one, the authenticity of the passage has been debated.

"I have taken a delight to publish in several places the hopes I have of Marie de Gournay le Jars, my adopted daughter; and certainly beloved by me more than paternally, and enveloped in my retirement and solitude as one of the best parts of my own being: I have no longer regard to anything in this world but her. And if a man may presage from her youth, her soul will one day be capable of very great things; and amongst others, of the perfection of that sacred friendship, to which we do not read that any of her sex could ever yet arrive." (II, 17)

The edition of the *Essays* edited and published by Mademoiselle de Gournay, originally preceded by a long preface signed by her, was the main version available for several centuries and was the one read, for example, by

Pascal and Rousseau. In the 20th century the quarto-sized "Bordeaux copy" became the preferred edition, as it was deemed more faithful to the 1588 edition Montaigne had covered with marginal annotations, or *allongeails* (elongations), as he called them. There are many differences between the Bordeaux copy and the 1595 edition, including the passage on Marie de Gournay, which is absent from the Bordeaux copy. However, there is now a renewed interest in the posthumous edition, as it is based on a better copy of the original text, and there is no longer any reason to doubt that Montaigne's lovely portrait of his adopted daughter is genuine:

"[ . . . ] the sincerity and solidity of her manners are already sufficient for it, and her affection towards me more than superabundant, and such, in short, as that there is nothing more to be wished, if not that the apprehension she has of my end, being now five-and-fifty years old, might not so much afflict her. The judgment she made of my first *Essays*, being a woman, so young, and in this age, and alone in her own country; and the famous vehemence wherewith she loved me, and desired my acquaintance solely from the esteem she had thence of me, before she ever saw my face, is an incident very worthy of consideration."

This relationship between an older man and a woman thirty years his junior has long been a source of curiosity. Montaigne had not had a friend in in the ideal, Classical sense of the word, since La Boétie's death in 1563; yet here he judges Mademoiselle de Gournay worthy of inclusion in the pantheon of the century's greatest individuals. A scholar of Greek, Latin, and Classical culture, de Gournay was far from being an "affected lady," as she has sometimes been called with disdain. She read the first two books of the *Essays* at the age of eighteen and was overwhelmed with admiration for their author. She met Montaigne just once, in Paris in 1588, and then corresponded with him until his death, before being asked by Madame de Montaigne to edit and publish the posthumous edition of the *Essays*.

In "Of Presumption," Montaigne, the father of six children, only one of whom—a daughter, Léonor—had survived, confides that he loves his adopted daughter "more than paternally," and as if she were a part of himself; he has "no longer regard to anything in this world but her." She, in return, has a "more than superabundant" affection for him. Their attachment proves, if such were needed, that Montaigne did not fall victim to his century's prejudices against women, for it was with a young woman, in the last years of his life, that he experienced an exceptional friendship, one worthy of Antiquity.

# 32

# THE HUNT AND THE CAPTURE

In the chapter "Upon Some Verses of Virgil," Montaigne, the upright, sincere, honest man who detests concealment above anything else, paradoxically rediscovers the delights of subtlety in matters of love. What he notes on this occasion is basically the difference between pornography, which shows everything, and eroticism, in which concealment is suggestive, serving to heighten desire:

"The more respectful, more timorous, more coy, and secret love of the Spaniards and Italians pleases me. I know not who of old wished his throat as long as that of a crane, that he might the longer taste what he swallowed; it had been better wished as to this quick and precipitous pleasure, especially in such natures as mine that have the fault of being too prompt. To stay its flight and delay it with preambles: all things—a glance, a bow, a word, a sign, stand for favour and recompense betwixt them. Were it not an excellent piece of thrift in him who could dine on the steam of the roast?" (III, 5)

Here, Montaigne sings the praises of taking love slowly, of seduction and gallantry, considered to be southern qualities. Even he, who can be "too prompt"—that is, unable to put off his own pleasures, understands that this is a case in which an overly direct and open manner does not pay. The charm of sensuality hinges on the lead-up to it. As for Montaigne's insistent equation of the pleasure of love to those of the table, it reminds us that lust and gluttony were—and are—vices; two of the seven cardinal sins, only aggravated by dilatory manoeuvres that delay their objective.

Deep down, Montaigne seems to have surprised even himself by unexpectedly embracing dissimulation and duplicity as he does here, despite condemning it everywhere else: "Let us teach the ladies to set a better value and esteem upon themselves, to amuse and fool us: we give the last charge at the first onset; the French impetuosity will still show itself." In this particular instance it falls to the ladies to induce men to conduct the foreplay of flirting slowly; to draw things out, to defer their favors.

Yet, the lesson Montaigne draws from this example applies much more broadly to our behaviour in life itself; it is one that softens his usual stance on forthrightness: "He who has no fruition but in fruition, who wins nothing unless he sweeps the stakes, who takes no pleasure in the chase but in the quarry, ought not to introduce himself in our school: the more steps and degrees there are, so much higher and more honourable is the uppermost seat: we should take a pleasure in being conducted to it, as in magnificent palaces, by various porticoes and passages, long and pleasant galleries, and many windings. [ . . . ] without hope and without desire we proceed not worth a pin."

When hunting, we take our pleasure not from the capture, but from the hunt itself, and from everything that goes along with it: the walking outside, the scenery, the company, the exercise. A hunter who thinks only of his prey is what we call "meathooked" (*un viandard*). And Montaigne says much the same about many other activities that are far less sensual; for example reading and study, and the spiritual "hunts" that exhaust us, in which the true moments of happiness are the ones we experience on the journey. Ours is the school of leisure, as Montaigne says; the *otium*, or retired, contemplative life, of the educated, thinking man, the hunter of books who can dedicate his time to an occupation with no immediate goal.

In the *Essays*, Montaigne displays an astonishing freedom in his writing. He rejects the artistic constraints of writing taught in school and unveils a loose and carefree style, which he analyses in the chapter "Of the Education of Children":

"I for my part rather bring in a fine sentence by head and shoulders to fit my purpose, than divert my designs to hunt after a sentence. On the contrary, words are to serve, and to follow a man's purpose; and let Gascon come in play where French will not do. I would have things so excelling, and so wholly possessing the imagination of him that hears, that he should have something else to do, than to think of words. The way of speaking that I love, is natural and plain, the same in writing as in speaking, and a sinewy and muscular way of expressing a man's self, short and pithy, not so elegant and artificial as prompt and vehement; [ . . . ] rather hard than wearisome; free from affectation; irregular, incontinuous, and bold; where every piece makes up an entire body; not like a pedant, a preacher, or a pleader, but rather a soldier-like style, as Suetonius calls that of Julius Caesar." (I, 25)

Montaigne does not like transitions or ornamentation;

he prefers to go straight to the point and rejects all stylistic effects. He refuses to use words to conceal things, to hide ideas beneath figurative language. For him, words are like clothing that must not distort the body, but rather mold to it like a leotard, allowing others to discern the shape underneath, emphasizing the natural lines. It is just one more say of rejecting artifice and make-up. Not only has Montaigne chosen to use French instead of Latin, but—if he cannot find the right French word—he does not hesitate to use the local patois. He is showcasing a way of writing that is as close as possible to the voice, "the same in writing as in speaking." The description of his ideal language is concrete, toothsome, physical. He uses sensual adjectives to evoke the style he admires most, and which has all the characteristics of brevity—the austere *brevitas* of the Spartans, as opposed to the *ubertas*, copious abundance, of the Athenians, at the risk of becoming a bit difficult to make out and verging on the enigmatic style of the Cretans. Instead of rhetorical eloquence, schooling, the pulpit, and the Bar—"a pedant, a preacher, or a pleader"—Montaigne favors the military elocution of Julius Caesar; his brisk, tight style composed of short, terse sentences, brief and to the point.

But Montaigne has another, more recent model in mind as well, one he has found in Baldassare Castiglione's fashionable *The Book of the Courtier*, published in 1528. This is what is called in Italian *sprezzatura*, the casual nonchalance of the courtier, the studied carelessness which, unlike affectation, conceals art.

"I have ever been ready to imitate the negligent garb,

which is yet observable amongst the young men of our time, to wear my cloak on one shoulder, my cap on one side, a stocking in disorder, which seems to express a kind of haughty disdain of these exotic ornaments, and a contempt of the artificial; but I find this negligence of much better use in the form of speaking. All affectation, particularly in the French gaiety and freedom, is ungraceful in a courtier, and in a monarchy every gentleman ought to be fashioned according to the court model; for which reason, an easy and natural negligence does well."

This is Montaigne's style: a cloak thrown over his shoulder; a cap tilted to one side, one stocking falling down—art meeting nature, at its finest.

Montaigne's thoughts on memory are extremely ambiguous. In keeping with Classical tradition, he continually sings memory's praises as a faculty indispensable to an accomplished man. Memory is the final part of rhetoric; thanks to it, the orator has a treasure trove of words and ideas allowing him to speak well under any circumstances. Every treatise on rhetoric, including those of Cicero and Quintilian, encourages the training of one's memory, and the Renaissance was the age of artificial memory and plays and spectacles based on memory. Yet Montaigne sets himself apart by insisting frequently on the poor quality of his memory, for example in the self-portrait he gives us in the chapter "Of Presumption":

"Memory is a faculty of wonderful use, and without which the judgment can very hardly perform its office: for my part I have none at all. What any one will propound to me, he must do it piecemeal, for to answer a speech consisting of several heads I am not able. I could not receive a commission by word of mouth without a note-book. And when I have a speech of consequence to make, if it be long, I am reduced to the miserable necessity of getting by heart word for word, what I am to say; I should otherwise have neither method nor assurance, being in fear that my memory would play me a slippery trick." (II, 17)

Montaigne claims that his memory is poor. This is only one of a long list of flaws that he rattles off every time he describes himself, in an attempt to show his physical and moral mediocrity. He is incapable of remembering complicated speeches, and thus of responding to them. If he is given a task it must be written down; and if he must retain a speech he has to memorize it and then regurgitate it mechanically. Montaigne reminds us again and again that he lacks the agile memory of the orator who, in order to remember his lengthy speeches, imagines himself as a building such as a house, the rooms of which he visits in his mind, recovering words and ideas from each of them that he has previously placed there. Montaigne's memory is not so agile, and thus he can only recite speeches he has committed to memory.

But the lack of a good memory has its advantages. First of all, it prevents lying and compels sincerity. A liar with a bad memory won't be able to remember what he has said, and to whom; he will inevitably contradict himself, soon exposing his deceit. Thus, Montaigne can announce his own honesty in all modesty; not as a virtue, but as a condition forced on him by his faulty memory. A man with no memory also has better judgment, because he depends less on others:

"Memory is the receptacle and case of science: and therefore mine being so treacherous, if I know little, I cannot much complain. I know, in general, the names of the arts, and of what they treat, but nothing more. I turn over books; I do not study them. What I retain I no longer recognise as another's; 'tis only what my judgment has made its advantage of, the discourses and imaginations in which it has been instructed: the author, place, words, and other circumstances, I immediately forget; and I am so excellent at forgetting, that I no less forget my own writings and compositions than the rest."

Simply put, Montaigne's profession of humility regarding his memory is also a claim to originality.

Montaigne is fascinated by small details in books that might seem unimportant to us, such as this one, in the brief chapter in Book One entitled "Of Smells":

"It has been reported of some, as of Alexander the Great, that their sweat exhaled an odoriferous smell, occasioned by some rare and extraordinary constitution, of which Plutarch and others have been inquisitive into the cause. But the ordinary constitution of human bodies is quite otherwise, and their best and chiefest excellency is to be exempt from smell." (I, 55)

Montaigne read about this minuscule trait in Plutarch's *Lives of the Noble Greeks and Romans*, his favorite bedtime book, and a Renaissance bestseller. First, this reminds us that odors could be torturously unpleasant in the era before modern hygiene; when Montaigne notes that the "ordinary constitution of human bodies is quite otherwise," what he means is that most people smelled awful. When Montaigne travels, he is irritated by the odors of the city: "My chiefest care in choosing my lodgings is always to avoid a thick and stinking air; and those beautiful cities, Venice and Paris, very much lessen the kindness I have for them, the one by the offensive smell of her marshes, and the other of her dirt."

The best we can hope for, usually, is for people not to smell of anything. Yet Alexander, with his delectable sweat, not only doesn't smell bad; he smells naturally good. According to Plutarch he had a hot and fiery temperament, which heated and dissipated the dampness of his body. Montaigne loved these kinds of observations, which he collected in his readings of historians. His interest lay not in great events, battles and conquests, but in personal anecdotes, mannerisms, impressions: Alexander cocked his head to one side; Cesar scratched his head with a finger; Cicero picked his nose. These involuntary gestures say more about a man than lofty discussions of his legend. They are what Montaigne looked for in his history books, as he says in the chapter "Of Books" in Book Two of the *Essays*, using an image borrowed from tennis, that of the "right ball," the easy ball that arrives in a straight shot:

"The historians are my right ball, for they are pleasant and easy, and where man, in general, the knowledge of whom I hunt after, appears more vividly and entire than anywhere else: the variety and truth of his internal qualities, in gross and piecemeal, the diversity of means by which he is united and knit, and the accidents that threaten him. Now those that write lives, by reason they insist more upon counsels than events, more upon what sallies from within, than upon what happens without, are the most proper for my reading" (II, 10)

In books by historians, Montaigne's favorite reading, he pays the most attention not to events, but to "counsels"—that is, to the deliberations that go into making these decisions; the way in which the decisions are made.

The outcome of events depends on fortune; the deliberations tell us more about the men, giving us a glimpse into
their minds.

"[ . . . ] and, therefore, above all others, Plutarch is the
man for me. I am very sorry we have not a dozen Laertii,—
[Diogenes Laertius, who wrote the *Lives of the
Philosophers*]—or that he was not further extended; for I
am equally curious to know the lives and fortunes of these
great instructors of the world, as to know the diversities of
their doctrines and opinions."

Montaigne, the hobbyist and connoisseur of lives, has
now set about writing the story of his own.

# 36
## AGAINST TORTURE

The case of Martin Guerre is a famous one. Guerre, a peasant, left his village following a family conflict. When he returned twelve years later a doppelgänger had taken his place, even in the marital bed. He filed a complaint. Lengthy legal proceedings followed to determine which of the two men was genuine. In 1560 the usurper, played onscreen by Gérard Depardieu in *Le Retour de Martin Guerre*, the 1982 film directed by Daniel Vigne, was found guilty and hanged. Jean de Coras, councillor to the Toulouse parliament, published the tale of this "prodigious story of our time," evoked by Montaigne in Book Three of the *Essays* in the chapter "Of Cripples":

"I read in my younger years a trial that Corras, a councillor of Toulouse, printed, of a strange incident, of two men who presented themselves the one for the other. I remember (and I hardly remember anything else) that he seemed to have rendered the imposture of him whom he judged to be guilty, so wonderful and so far exceeding both our knowledge and his own, who was the judge, that I thought it a very bold sentence that condemned him to be hanged. Let us have some form of decree that says, 'The court understands nothing of the matter' more freely and ingenuously than the Areopagites did, who, finding themselves perplexed with a cause they could not unravel, ordered the parties to appear again after a hundred years." (III, 11)

Montaigne mixes up the years—he was twenty-seven at the time, no longer a child—but admits his perplexity. If he had been in Coras's place, he could not have chosen between the two Martins or decided who was the real one and the false one; the one who had lived for years with his young wife and family, or the one who had come back after a long absence and reclaimed his place. The episode of the supposed Martin Guerre seems so "wonderful" to Montaigne that he finds the judge's condemnation of the pretender extremely daring, and he would have preferred—like the Areopagites when faced with an unsolvable case—for judgment to be suspended.

Montaigne's interest in Martin Guerre extends to other difficult or impossible-to-untangle affairs as well. He takes a stand against the torture that is sometimes resorted to in an attempt to resolve them; witches, for example, in the case of which he—almost alone in his era—abstains from judgment:

"The witches of my neighbourhood run the hazard of their lives upon the report of every new author who seeks to give body to their dreams. [ . . . ] that we neither see the causes nor the means, will require another sort-of wit than ours. [ . . . ] To kill men, a clear and strong light is required, [ . . . ] and I am of St. Augustine's opinion, that, ''tis better to lean towards doubt than assurance, in things hard to prove and dangerous to believe'."

The fashion in Montaigne's time was for treatises on demonology, which claimed to explain the phenomena of black magic and justified the use of torture in witch trials. Montaigne remains skeptical; for him, witches are mad, and demonologists are impostors; both the former and the latter are victims of the same collective illusion. Our ignorance should lead us to greater caution and reserve. "After all," he concludes, "'tis setting a man's conjectures at a very high price upon them to cause a man to be roasted alive."

Faced with the false Martin Guerre, witches, and even Indians from the New World (in the chapter "Of Coaches"), Montaigne stands against all forms of cruelty and urges tolerance and indulgence. Few sentiments define him better than that.

Every time Montaigne touches on religious matters, he does so with extreme caution; for example, in the opening lines of the chapter "Of Prayers" in Book One of the *Essays*, when he gives his opinion on this ritual Christian act:

"I propose formless and undetermined fancies, like those who publish doubtful questions, to be after disputed upon in the schools, not to establish truth but to seek it; and I submit them to the judgments of those whose office it is to regulate, not my writings and actions only, but moreover my very thoughts. Let what I here set down meet with correction or applause, it shall be of equal welcome and utility to me, myself beforehand condemning as absurd and impious, if anything shall be found, through ignorance or inadvertency, couched in this rhapsody, contrary to the holy resolutions and prescriptions of the Catholic Apostolic and Roman Church, into which I was born and in which I will die." (I, 56)

The chapter begins, once again, with a profession of humility. These are simply idle discussions in which we are not trying to come to any conclusions; we are debating for the sheer pleasure of it, as one might do at university. We can argue for a theory just as easily as we can argue against it; *pro et contra, sic et non*. We are exercising our minds, not promulgating laws. This is true of all the *Essays*; they are thought exercises or experiments. Montaigne is playing with ideas, not writing treatises on philosophy of theology. He is not wedded to his propositions; he declares that he would refute them willingly if they were found to be mistaken, and submits himself unreservedly to the authority of the Church.

This would be the purpose of his voyage to Rome in 1580, which he took in order to submit Books One and Two of the *Essays* to pontifical censure. The Church criticized many small details, such as the use of the word *fortune*, but did not object, for example, to the book's mentions of fideism or Christian skepticism, the near-absolute separation of faith from reason, as discussed in "Apology for Raimond Sebond." And from 1588 onward, Montaigne, sensing the approach of death, added material to the beginning of "Of Prayers" to emphasize his attachment to the Church.

However, none of this prevents him from making numerous allusions to his distrust of miracles and superstitions, or, as we have seen, to advocate greater tolerance for those accused of witchcraft in his area. There are also more troubling remarks to be found tucked away here and there in the *Essays*, such as this one in "Apology":

"What I hold and believe to-day I hold and believe with my whole belief; all my instruments and engines seize and take hold of this opinion, and become responsible to me for it, at least as much as in them lies; I could not embrace nor conserve any truth with greater confidence and assurance than I do this; I am wholly and entirely possessed with it; but has it not befallen me, not only once, but a hundred, a thousand times, every day, to have embraced some other thing with all the same instruments, and in the same condition, which I have since judged to be false?" (II, 12)

In other words, I can believe something right now, with all my heart and with total and complete sincerity and confidence, while knowing at the same time that my beliefs often change. Uncertainty of judgment and inconstancy of actions are key themes in the *Essays*, strategically repeated again and again. In speaking of his beliefs, Montaigne does not make explicit reference to the Christian faith, but it cannot be exempt from his habitual changeability unless we see it as something completely different, which would not be in keeping with the character of the man.

# 38

# KNOWLEDGEABLE IGNORANCE

Toward the end of Book One of the *Essays*, at the beginning of the chapter "Of Democritus and Heraclitus"—the philosopher who laughs and the one who weeps, two ways of expressing the absurdity of the human condition—Montaigne takes stock of his own methods:

"I leave the choice of my arguments to fortune, and take that she first presents to me; they are all alike to me, I never design to go through any of them." (I, 50)

In other words: "Every subject is equally fertile to me" (III, 5). Montaigne's contemplative process can start with any observation, reading, or chance encounter. This is why he adores travelling so much; especially horseback riding, as we have seen, during which he has his best ideas, which are inspired and then sustained by the motion of things, of life. He follows one train of thought for a while and then abandons it for another, which is all right, because everything is related.

This brief discussion of his method is followed by a lengthier addition later:

"[ . . . ] for I never see all of anything: neither do they who so largely promise to show it others. Of a hundred members and faces that everything has, I take one, while to look it over only, another while to ripple up the skin, and sometimes to pinch it to the bones: I give a stab, not so wide but as deep as I can, and am for the most part tempted to take it in hand by some new light I discover in it." (I, 50)

Now, after having published his *Essays*, Montaigne is more self-assured. Those who claim to get to the bottom of things, he says, are deceiving us, for man cannot understand the bottom of things. And the diversity of the world is so great that all knowledge is fragile; mere opinion, really. Things have "a hundred members and faces," and "their most universal quality is diversity" (II, 37); so much so, in fact, that all I can claim is to shed some light on one of their aspects or another. Montaigne has multiple points of view; he contradicts himself, but this is because the world itself is full of paradoxes and inconsistencies.

"Did I know myself less, I might perhaps venture to handle something or other to the bottom, and to be deceived in my own inability; but sprinkling here one word and there another, patterns cut from several pieces and scattered without design and without engaging myself too far, I am not responsible for them, or obliged to keep close to my subject, without varying at my own liberty and pleasure, and giving up myself to doubt and uncertainty, and to my own governing method, ignorance." (I, 50)

Only delusion can make us believe that we have understood a subject to its very bottom. Skipping from one subject to another, taking everything in small morsels, Montaigne does not write as if he intends his work to be permanent, serious, definitive; rather, he follows his own whims, contradicting himself on occasion, or suspending judgment if the subject is obdurate or indecipherable—witchcraft, for example.

The additional passage concludes by praising ignorance, "my own governing method." But, be careful: this ignorance, which is the final lesson of the *Essays*, is not the primitive ignorance, the "stupidity and ignorance," of a person who refuses to understand and does not strive for awareness; it is knowledgeable ignorance, which has learned and studied, and realized that we can only ever know anything halfway. There is nothing worse in the world than people with half-knowledge, as Pascal would describe it—people who believe they are wise. The ignorance Montaigne is commending here is that of Socrates, who knows that he knows nothing; it is "the extreme degree of perfection and difficulty" united with "the pure and first impression and ignorance of nature." (III, 12)

# 39

# Wasted Time

In the margins of the Bordeaux copy of the *Essays*, the large quarto edition of 1588 that Montaigne filled with "elongations" until his death in 1592, there are many reflections made in hindsight, such as this addition to the chapter "Of Giving the Lie":

"And though nobody should read me, have I wasted time in entertaining myself so many idle hours in so pleasing and useful thoughts? In moulding this figure upon myself, I have been so often constrained to temper and compose myself in a right posture, that the copy is truly taken, and has in some sort formed itself; painting myself for others, I represent myself in a better colouring than my own natural complexion. I have no more made my book than my book has made me: 'tis a book consubstantial with the author, of a peculiar design, a parcel of my life, and whose business is not designed for others, as that of all other books is." (II, 18)

Of what use are the *Essays*? What makes Montaigne so human, so much like us, is doubt—including self-doubt. He hesitates frequently, caught between laughter and sadness. At the *Essays'* conclusion, this man who has dedicated the greater part of his life to them is still wondering if he has wasted his time. The book is put forth as a mold, like an impression taken of a model in order to reproduce its contours. But Montaigne goes further, not content with this simple analogy; he describes a dialectic which binds the original and the reproduction, the "figure" and the "copy," to use his terms. The act of molding has transformed the model, which emerges better "tempered"; that is, better styled and put together. The model sees itself in the copy, but the copy has changed the model. They have made each other, so much so that they have become indistinguishable, the line between them blurred: "who touches the one, touches the other," Montaigne says in the chapter "Of Repentance" (III, 2).

We sense that he feels a certain sense of pride at having succeeded in an unprecedented undertaking; no author before him had ever attempted such complete identification between man and book. But even this small touch of vanity must soon be given up, for everything happened without intent, by chance, according to whim.

"In giving myself so continual and so exact an account of myself, have I lost my time? For they who sometimes cursorily survey themselves only, do not so strictly examine themselves, nor penetrate so deep, as he who makes it his business, his study, and his employment, who intends a lasting record, with all his fidelity, and with all his force. [ ... ] How often has this work diverted me from troublesome thoughts?" (II, 18)

Montaigne is aware that his approach is both unique and daring; people who examine themselves only in thought and speech, or merely on occasion, cannot gain as deep an understanding of the self, and thus of mankind. Montaigne knows that writing, and writing about himself, have changed him, both in himself and with regard to others. "That such a man as Montaigne wrote has truly augmented the joy of living on this earth," observed Nietzsche.

But there is no question of "form[ing] a statue to erect in the great square of a city" (II, 18); as soon as he has put himself forward a bit, Montaigne draws back. Above all, writing has been a distraction, a remedy for boredom, a defense against melancholy.

# 40

# THE THRONE OF THE WORLD

I wondered for a long time if I would dare to cite the irreverent conclusion of the *Essays*, at the risk of offending delicate ears. But if Montaigne said it, what right do I have to avoid repeating it? So, because this will be my last, here we go: "Aesop, that great man, saw his master piss as he walked: 'What then,' said he, 'must we drop as we run?' Let us manage our time; there yet remains a great deal idle and ill employed." (III, 13)

An entire philosophy of life is summed up in these few, startling sentences. Men in the Renaissance did not set as much store by manners as we do; they said frankly what they were thinking. The last chapter of the *Essays*, "Of Experience," gives us Montaigne's final piece of wisdom, often associated with Epicureanism. We should take the time to live; follow nature, and enjoy the present, for hurrying is pointless. *Festina lente*, or "make haste slowly," as a paradoxical motto favored by Erasmus has it. As Montaigne expresses it a bit earlier in the text:

"I have a special vocabulary of my own; I 'pass away time,' when it is ill and uneasy, but when 'tis good I do not pass it away: 'I taste it over again and adhere to it'; one must run over the ill and settle upon the good."

We can hurry through life when it is difficult, but we must also savor the pleasures of the moment in tranquillity. *Carpe diem*, as Horace said. "Seize the day; put very little trust in tomorrow"; take advantage of the present in all its richness without thinking of death. The final pages of the *Essays* repeat this moral in a multitude of forms, urging a life lived in the here and now:

"When I dance, I dance; when I sleep, I sleep. Nay, when I walk alone in a beautiful orchard, if my thoughts are some part of the time taken up with external occurrences, I some part of the time call them back again to my walk, to the orchard, to the sweetness of that solitude, and to myself."

The moral code of life proposed by Montaigne is also an aesthetic; it is the art of living in beauty. The seizure of a moment becomes a way of being truly present in the world; modest, natural, simply and completely human.

"The pretty inscription wherewith the Athenians honoured the entry of Pompey into their city is conformable to my sense: 'By so much thou art a god, as thou confessest thee a man.' 'Tis an absolute and, as it were, a divine perfection, for a man to know how loyally to enjoy his being. We seek other conditions, by reason we do not understand the use of our own; and go out of ourselves, because we know not how there to reside. 'Tis to much purpose to go upon stilts, for, when upon stilts, we must yet walk with our legs; and when seated upon the most elevated throne in the world, we are but seated upon our breech. The fairest lives, in my opinion, are those which regularly accommodate themselves to the common and human model without miracle, without extravagance."

The final words of the *Essays* accept life as it is given to us and whatever it may have in store for us, and this applies to everyone; the great and the humble, because in the face of death we are all equal. Montaigne even finds it in himself to reproach Socrates, his ultimate hero, for having wished to escape the human condition, having a demon tugging at his sleeve like a guardian angel. Montaigne himself is naked, open to nature, approving his own fate. He is our brother.

## About the Author

Antoine Compagnon is a Professor of French Literature at Collège de France, Paris, and the Blanche W. Knopf Professor of French and Comparative Literature at Columbia University, New York. He is a member of the American Academy of Arts and Sciences, and holds honorary degrees from King's College London, HEC Paris, and the University of Liège.